LOW COST SHORE PROTECTION

... a Guide for Engineers and Contractors

The U. S. Army Corps of Engineers presents this information as a public service. Inclusion of any shore protection device or method does not necessarily constitute a government recommendation or endorsement, nor is it guaranteed that any particular method will be successful for a specific application.

TABLE OF CONTENTS

TABLE OF CONTENTS
(Continued)

LOW COST SHORE PROTECTION

... a Guide for Engineers and Contractors

INTRODUCTION

The purpose of this report is to familiarize engineers and contractors with various established methods of low cost shore protection. It is written for the individual who is knowledgeable in general civil engineering design and construction, but not a specialist in coastal engineering or shoreline protection. This report can be used without other references, but many topics are discussed with only minimal detail, so some additional reading may be necessary to gain a better understanding of the text. The *Suggested Reading* section at the end of the report lists a full range of readily available books, reports, and publications that are recommended for additional background study.

LOW COST SHORE PROTECTION

In distinguishing between *low cost* and cheap, one should remember that practically any method of shore protection, if properly implemented, is expensive. Significant investments are required to achieve the durability needed to resist even small waves. Low cost simply means that the various measures are commensurate with the value of individual residential or commercial properties. The total cost of implementation will vary with the different alternatives, but in all cases, there should be a suitable (and affordable) range of solutions.

The methods described in this report are usually appropriate for use only in sheltered waters. That is, they are generally not intended for open coast sites where they would be exposed to the undiminished attack of large oceanic waves. *Use of most of these structures in such areas is definitely not recommended and entails a considerable risk of failure.*

THE SHORELINE EROSION CONTROL DEMONSTRATION PROGRAM

From 1975 to 1980, the U. S. Army Corps of Engineers conducted a program to develop and demonstrate low cost methods of shore protection. This program was mandated by Section 54 of Public Law 93-251, the Shoreline Erosion Control Demonstration Act of 1974. Working with the Soil Conservation Service, the Corps designated 16 demonstration sites throughout the Atlantic, Gulf, and Pacific coasts, Alaska and the Great Lakes. These sites were chosen because they represented a broad cross section of shoreform and environmental conditions. This would permit wide application of the results obtained to other sites located throughout the country. At each of these sites, various structures and kinds of vegetation were established to evaluate their effectiveness in the local environment. Twenty-one additional supplemental sites were also chosen where existing shore protection devices had previously been established by others.

The devices at all 37 sites were intensively monitored over a period of months. Data that were collected included daily visual observations of wave heights and directions, quarterly surveys of beach and offshore profiles, quarterly color aerial photos, quarterly sediment sampling and gradation analyses, and monthly site visits with ground level photos.

SHORELINE PROCESSES

Before developing a comprehensive solution for a client, it is first necessary to understand the coastal processes that are contributing to the erosion problem. The following sections present basic information about shoreline processes that will serve as a foundation for later discussions. These sections are not exhaustive in their depth of coverage and cannot replace detailed and widely accepted texts such as the <u>Shore Protection Manual</u> [U.S. Army Corps of Engineers (1977c)].

<u>Wave Action</u>

While waves are always present on the open coast, they are not continuous in sheltered waters. Nonetheless, they are still the major cause of erosion in these areas. Several basic wave characteristics are important. The wave height is the vertical distance between the wave crest and trough, the period is the time (in seconds) it takes two successive wave crests to pass a stationary point, and the wavelength is the distance between successive crests (Figure 1). Using linear wave theory (the simplest case), these characteristics are given by the expressions;

$$L = CT \qquad (1)$$

where L = wavelength in feet,
          C = wave celerity (speed) in feet/second,
and T = wave period in seconds;

$$C = (gT/2\pi) \tanh (2\pi d/L) \qquad (2)$$

Where d = water depth in feet;
And g = acceleration due to gravity, 32.2 ft/sec^2

And

$$L = (gT^2/2\pi) \tanh (2\pi d/L) \qquad (3)$$

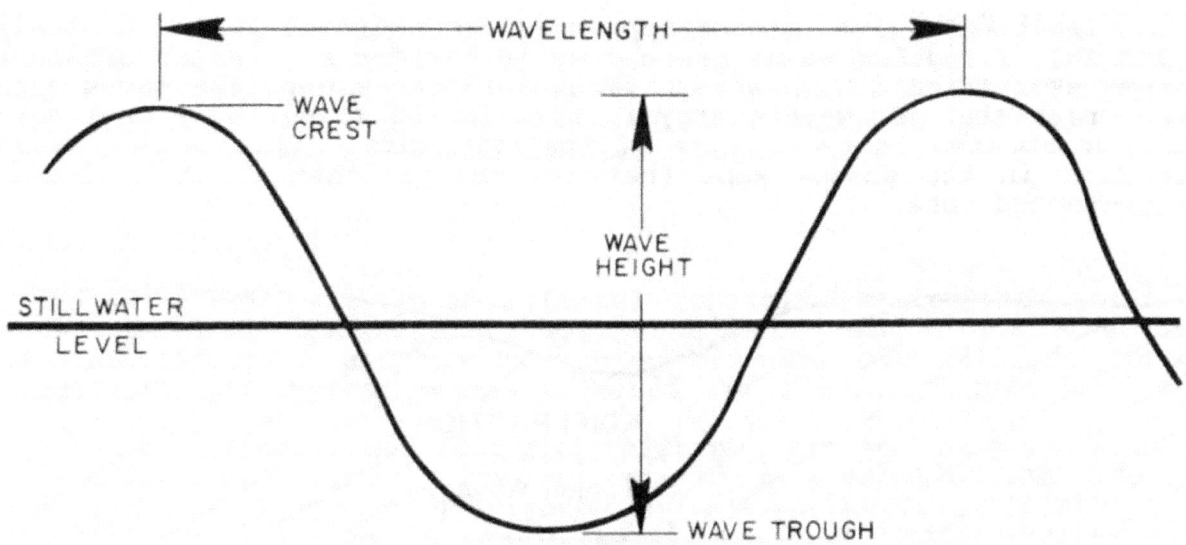

WAVE PERIOD IS THE TIME REQUIRED FOR SUCCESSIVE CRESTS TO PASS A STATIONARY POINT.

Figure 1   Characteristics of Waves

As a wave moves through deep water (depths greater than one-half the wavelength), the celerity and wavelength remain essentially constant, because for d/L > 0.5 (deep water); the expression tanh [2πd/L] approaches unity. Therefore, since the period remains constant, the celerity and wavelength also do not vary. However, when a wave approaches the shallower water near the shore (where d/L <0.5), Equations (2) and (3) cannot be simplified by ignoring tanh [2π/L]. From Equation (2), the celerity decreases with depth; the wave slows as it enters shallower water. The same is true with the wavelength, L, as can be seen from Equation (3), where it appears on both sides of the equation and an iterative solution is required.

As the wave continues to move in shoaling water, its profile begins to steepen and its gently rolling shape changes to a series of sharp crests with intervening flat troughs. At some point, this process can continue no longer and the wave breaks at the shore. The break point is a function of the wave height; period, water depth and bottom slope, but as a first approximation, assume that the wave breaks when the height is about 0.78 times the depth. For example, a 5-foot high wave breaks in a water depth of about 6.4 feet.

Important wave properties are demonstrated when a train (series) of regular waves meets a solid barrier such as an offshore breakwater,(Figure 2). Wave diffraction occurs when the waves pass the breakwater and wave energy is transferred along their crests to the quiet area in the shadow of the structure. This causes waves to form in the shadow zone that are smaller than in the adjacent unprotected zone.

Wave reflection occurs on the offshore side of the breakwater. While waves passing the structure are diffracted, the portions striking the breakwater are reflected like a billiard ball from a cushion. If the structure is a smooth vertical wall, the reflection is nearly perfect; and if the wave crests are parallel with the breakwater, the reflected and incident waves will reinforce each other to form standing waves twice as high as the incident waves. This could cause considerable bottom scour at the toe of, and offshore from, the structure. If the waves approach at an angle, no standing waves will form, but the resulting water surface, with crossing wave crests, will be rough and choppy. These short-crested waves could also cause considerable bottom scour.

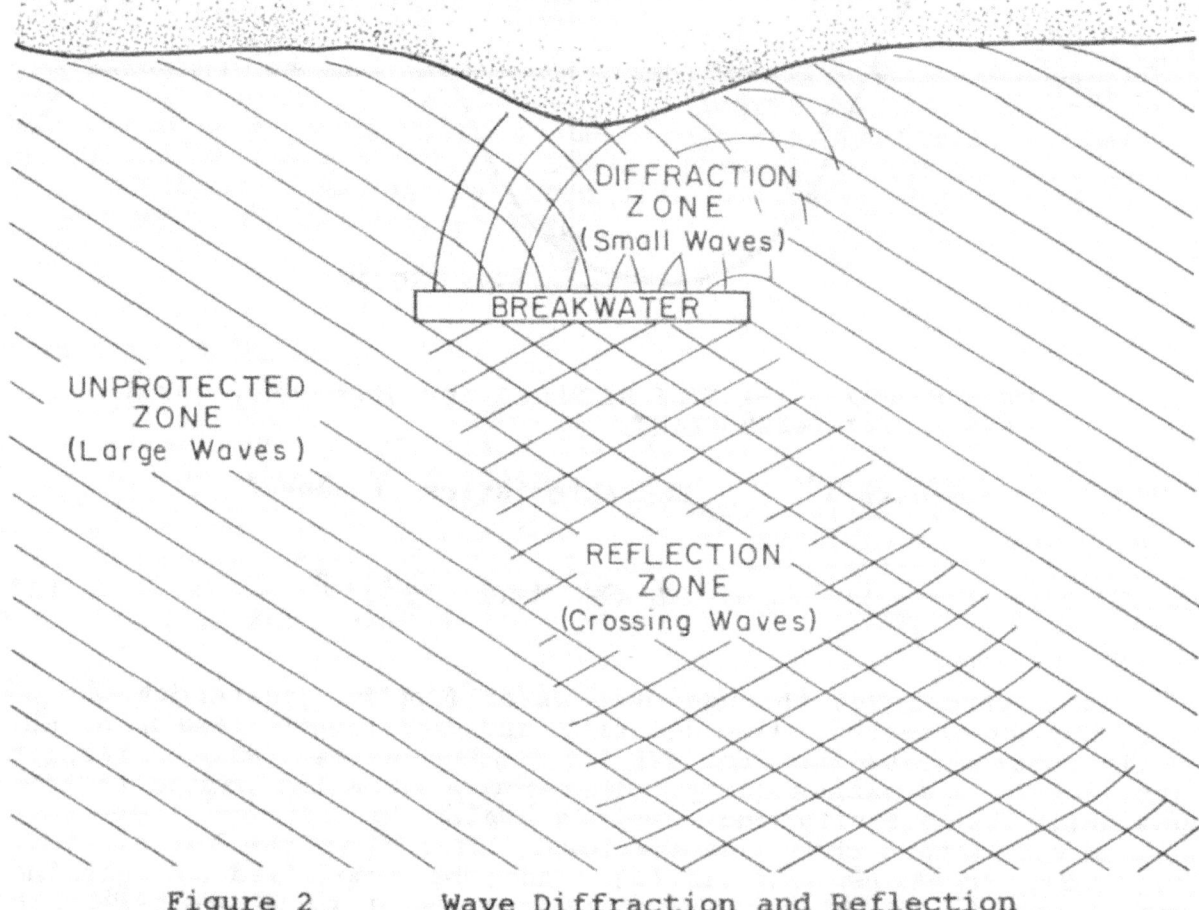

Figure 2   Wave Diffraction and Reflection

The final important wave characteristic is evident when waves break either on a beach or structure. The uprush of water after breaking is called runup and it expends the wave's remaining energy. The runup height depends on the roughness and steepness of the structure or beach and the characteristics of the wave. In general, increased roughness reduces runup.

Sediment Transport

The large variety of littoral (shoreline) materials include rock, boulders, cobbles, gravels, sand, silt, and clay. A number of classification systems have been developed to identify these materials, and typical scales of sizes are given in Figure 3.

Rock characterizes cliff shorelines, such as along the coasts of northern California. Boulders are often present at the base of such cliffs because of rock fracturing and weathering. Cobbles and gravels are prevalent beach materials in the Pacific Northwest, Alaska, and the Great Lakes area. Sand, the most common shoreline material, is found in virtually all coastal areas. Silts and clays generally occur on bluff shorelines or marshes, such as along the Great Lakes and various bays.

Littoral materials are derived from the deterioration and erosion of coastal bluffs and cliffs; the weathering of rock materials found inland and transported to the shore by rivers and streams; the disintegration of shells, coral or algae to form carbonate materials; and the production of organic material (generally peat) by coastal marshes and wetlands.

Failure or erosion of a bluff causes material to be deposited at the base. Waves sort this material and carry the fine-grained silts and clays offshore where they settle to the bottom. The original deposit is eventually reduced to sand and gravel fractions, which form a beach. Eventually, if no other littoral material is carried to the site by waves, even the sand and fine gravel will disappear down the coast or offshore, leaving only coarse gravels behind. However, a new supply of material may be deposited on the beach by a fresh failure of the bluff, and the process begins again. In many cases, therefore, the littoral materials comprising beaches are often derived from erosion of the shoreline itself.

Rivers and streams that carry sediments eroded from the inland land mass are a second source of littoral material, particularly during floods. Material from this source is predominantly smaller than sand, particularly for large rivers. These silts and clays are largely deposited far offshore. Smaller rivers that flow through sandy drainage areas may carry significant quantities of sand during floods. However, the total contribution of sand by rivers and streams is probably considerably less than from erosion of the shores themselves.

Coral reefs, shells, and other plant or animal matter are a third material source. They gradually break and weather into carbonate sands, which are, for instance, the primary components of beaches south of Palm Beach, Florida. Swamps, marshes, and coastal wetlands produce peats and other organic matter, also a source of littoral material. Too light to remain in place under continued wave action, they are ultimately washed offshore unless stabilized.

Littoral materials are transported along the shore by wave action. Approaching from deeper water, the shoreward portion of a wave moves in progressively more shallow water than the section farther of f shore. This portion begins to slow, which causes the wave to bend (refract) until breaking at an angle to the beach. This creates considerable turbulence that temporarily suspends the bottom sediments and carries them up the foreshore (beach face) in the general direction of wave advance. The motion stops a short distance up the beach, and then reverses direction back down the slope. However, the downrush does not retrace the same path, but rather, moves directly down the foreshore in response to gravity. The next wave repeats the process, moving the material downdrift along the beach.

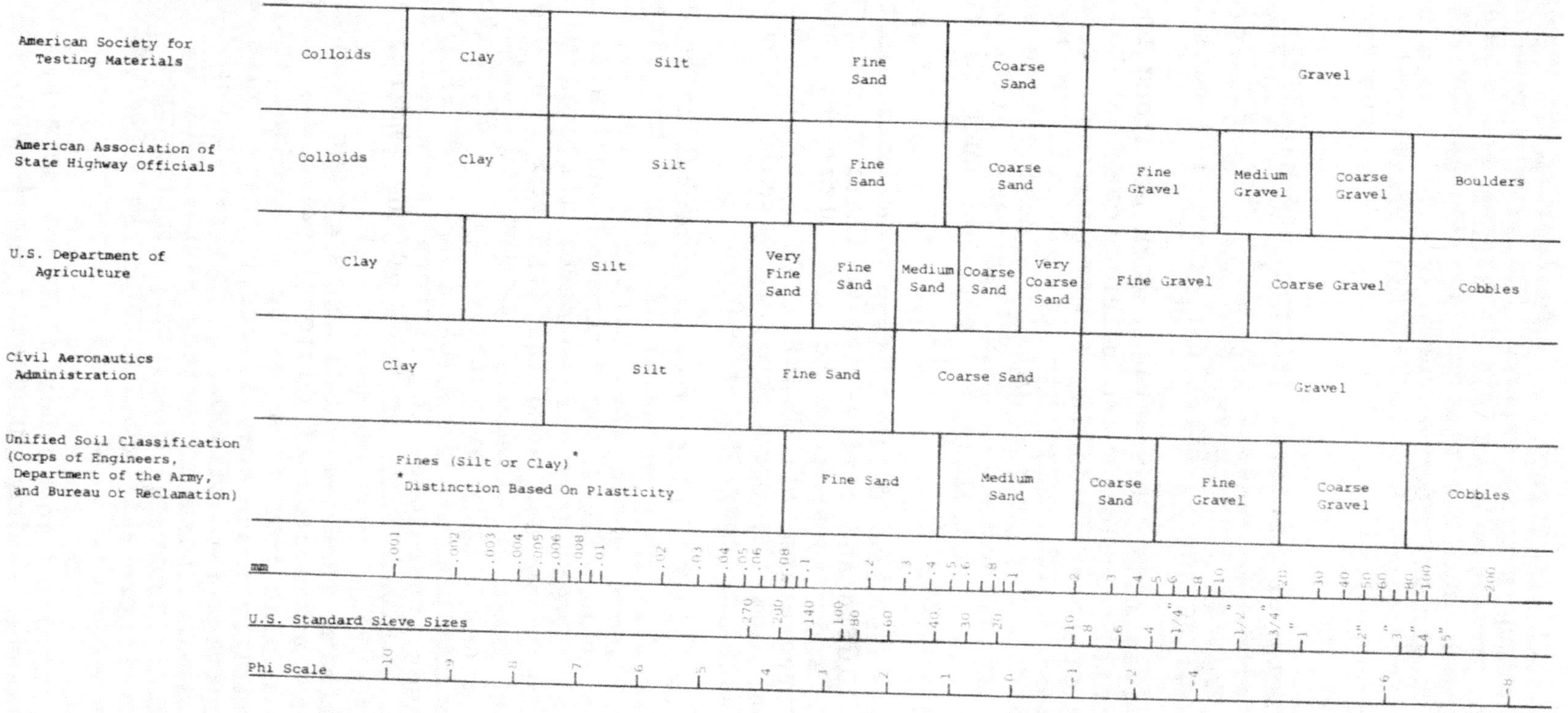

American Society for Testing Materials: Colloids | Clay | Silt | Fine Sand | Coarse Sand | Gravel

American Association of State Highway Officials: Colloids | Clay | Silt | Fine Sand | Coarse Sand | Fine Gravel | Medium Gravel | Coarse Gravel | Boulders

U.S. Department of Agriculture: Clay | Silt | Very Fine Sand | Fine Sand | Medium Sand | Coarse Sand | Very Coarse Sand | Fine Gravel | Coarse Gravel | Cobbles

Civil Aeronautics Administration: Clay | Silt | Fine Sand | Coarse Sand | Gravel

Unified Soil Classification (Corps of Engineers, Department of the Army, and Bureau of Reclamation): Fines (Silt or Clay)* *Distinction Based On Plasticity | Fine Sand | Medium Sand | Coarse Sand | Fine Gravel | Coarse Gravel | Cobbles

U.S. Standard Sieve Sizes

Phi Scale

Figure 3   Common Soil Classification Systems
[After Winterkorn and Fang (1975)]

Littoral transport occurs not only by rolling bedload, as above, but also by the movement of suspended sediment. The waves generate a longshore current that flows through the area where they break (breaker zone). Alone, it is generally too weak to move appreciable quantities of sediment; however, the turbulence from breaking waves suspends sediments that can then be moved downdrift by the longshore current. This sediment generally settles out within a short distance, but the next wave provides additional movement. Therefore, longshore transport is caused by the zig-zag movement of bedload up and down the beach, and the turbulence and action of the wave-induced longshore current.

Water Level Variations

The water surface elevation itself constantly changes with time. The Stillwater level, or the water level with no waves present, changes because of three processes; astronomical tides, storms, and periodic lake level variations.

Astronomical Tides - Tides are generated by the gravitational attraction between the earth, moon, and sun, and are classified as diurnal, semidiurnal, or mixed. Diurnal tides have only one high and one low each lunar day. Semidiurnal tides have two approximately equal highs and two approximately equal lows daily. Mixed tides are intermediate between them and typically have two highs and lows that occur each day. However, in contrast to semidiurnal tides, there is a large inequality, or difference in height, between either successive high or successive low waters (Figure 4). Most Atlantic coast tides are semidiurnal and the heights of successive highs or lows are approximately equal. Gulf and Pacific coast tides tend to be mixed, and in most cases, there is a distinct inequality between successive highs or lows.

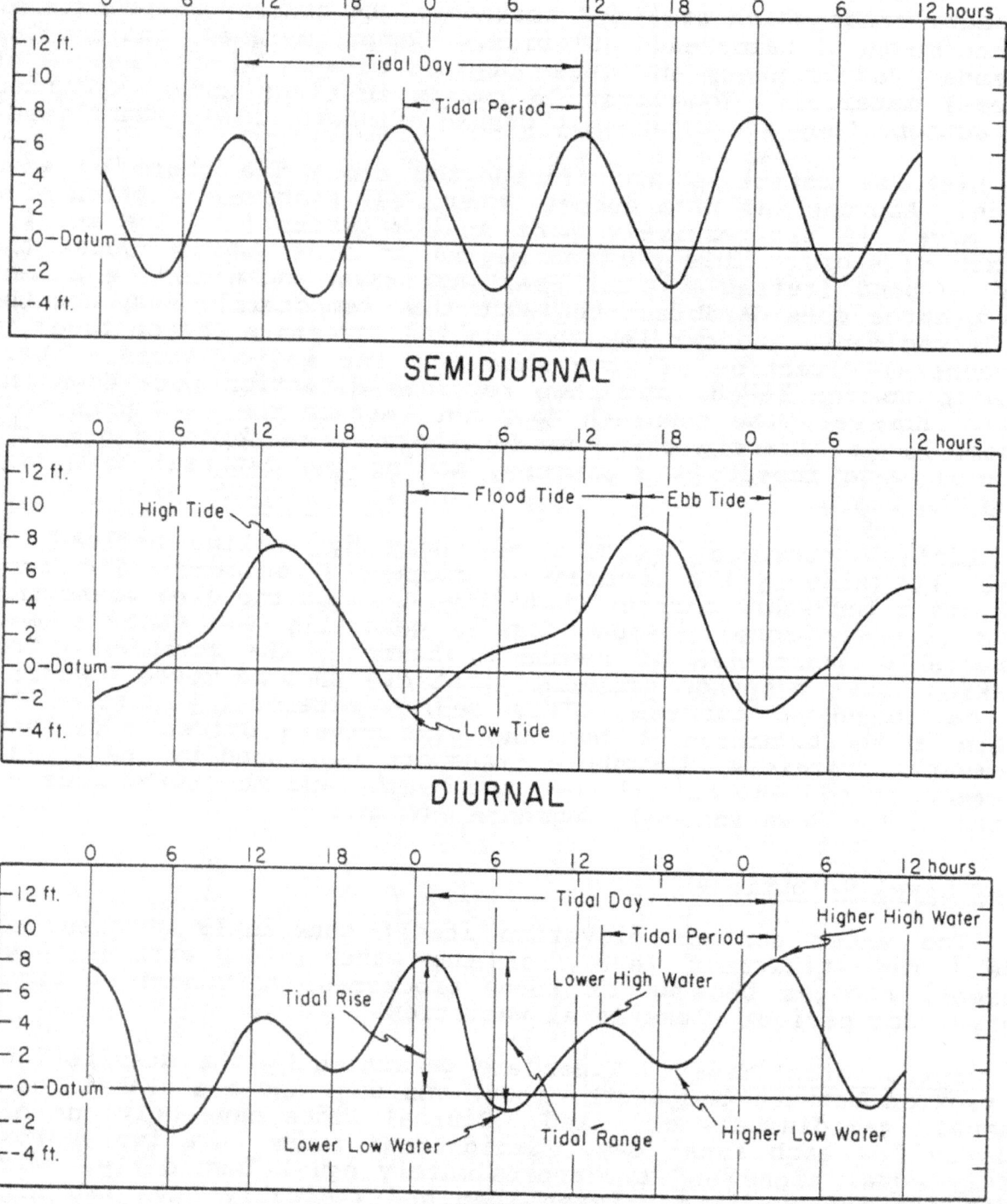

Figure 4   Types of Tides
[Wiegel (1953)]

In addition, the tidal range, or difference in elevation between the high and low waters, tends to fluctuate throughout the month. These tidal range variations are caused by changes in the distance between the earth and moon (perigean and apogean tides), the declination of the moon (equatorial and tropical tides), the declination of the sun, and the phase of the moon (spring or neap tides). *(See Glossary.)* The tides are highest during spring, perigean and tropical tides and are particularly high when these are approximately in phase.

Tides are also present on the Great Lakes, but they are small and not significant for practical problems of shore protection design.

Some key tidal datums, shown on Figure 5, are important because of their wide use. Not shown are datums for the Great Lakes, where all levels are ultimately referenced to the International Great Lakes Datum (see *Glossary*). Each lake has a designated chart datum [Low Water Datum (LWD)] based on the IGLD.

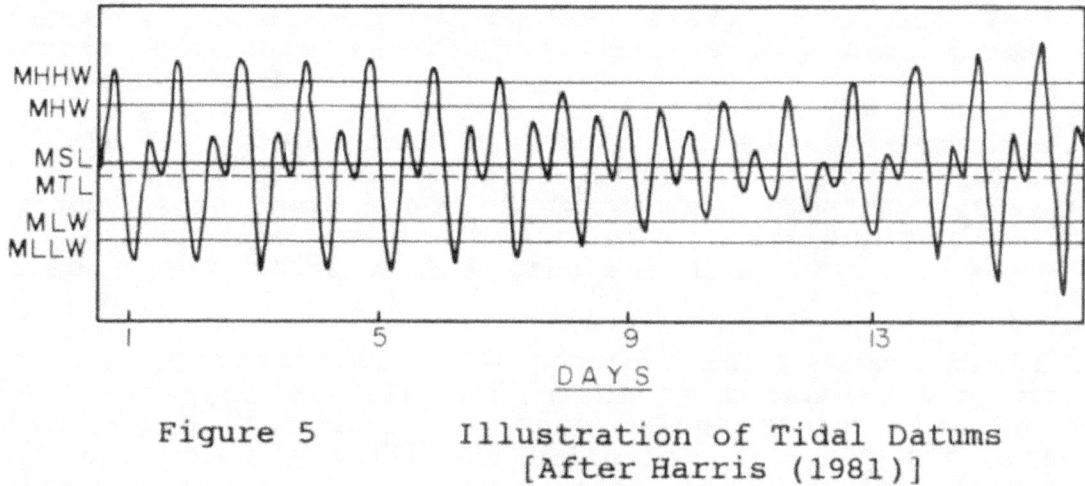

Figure 5   Illustration of Tidal Datums
[After Harris (1981)]

Storm Effects. The passage of storms tends to increase the Stillwater level through two principal mechanisms: atmospheric pressure effects, and stress caused by storm winds blowing across the water. Atmospheric pressure differences across a large water body cause a rise in the water level in the lower pressure area (inverse barometer effect). Water surface rises of one or two feet are common in many areas under this effect.

Enclosed water bodies (such as the Great Lakes) can also respond to storm forces by seiching. This occurs when storm winds or pressure effects drive the water surface higher at the downwind end of a lake. The passage of the storm front releases this water, and causes a periodic oscillation within the basin that will continue for several cycles. On the Great Lakes, seiching is most pronounced on Erie, because its long axis more closely matches predominant storm tracks and its relatively shallow depths lead to higher storm setup levels.

Wind stress also tends to drive the water on shore to above normal heights (storm setup). This continues until the tendency for the water to flow back to its normal level balances the forces driving it on shore. The high winds associated with storms also generate large waves, with their effects being felt in addition to the elevated storm surge levels.

Lake Level Variations.   Water levels in the Great Lakes are also subject to periodic changes. Records of lake levels dating from 1836 reveal seasonal and annual changes, which are due to variations in precipitation annually, and from year to year.   Lake levels (particularly Ontario and Superior) are also partially controlled by regulatory works operated jointly by Canadian and U. S. authorities, and these may result in minimizing lake level changes.   Average monthly lake level elevations showing data for the past calendar year and present year to date, and a forecast for the next six months, are published monthly by the U. S. Army Corps of Engineers, Detroit District (see *Other Help* Section).

THE EROSION PROBLEM

THE IMPORTANCE OF SHOREFORM

The land-sea boundary in characterized by many shapes and configurations. Geologists have devised elaborate classification systems to describe these various features. For the purposes of understanding basic shoreline processes and for designing appropriate corrective measures, however, it will only be necessary to informally classify shorelines as either bluffs, low erodible plains (including sandy beaches), or wetlands. Many shorelines, of course, contain two or even all three of these basic features.

Bluff Shorelines

A distinction will be drawn between bluffs and cliffs. Cliffs will be defined as shorelines composed of relatively sound rock. These rarely undergo severe or sudden erosion problems, but may experience slow, steady retreat over a long period of years. Such shorelines generally cannot be treated with low cost solutions because available alternatives are usually less durable than the cliff rock itself.

On the other hand, bluffs are composed of sediments such as clay, sand, gravel, or erodible rock and erosion problems are often present along these kinds of shorelines. The most prevalent causes of bluff erosion are toe scour by wave action, surface runoff, and drainage and infiltration problems that lead to slope stability failures.

An important factor to consider is whether a bluff is high or low. While no precise definition is possible, many writers have described high bluffs as those being greater than 20 or 30 feet high or, using a different criterion, a low bluff might be classified as one that can stand alone, while a high bluff must either be protected, or otherwise treated, to remain standing.

In evaluating conditions at a site, it is necessary to determine which of the above processes is primarily responsible for the erosion problem. Slope stability problems that are not aggravated by toe undercutting should be treated using established civil engineering techniques of slope stability analysis and design. Typical solutions could include vertical or horizontal drains, slope regrading and terracing, surface drainage controls, elimination of unnecessary surcharges at the top of the slope, and buttressing the toe.

Wave action at the toe which undermines the bluff, can be treated using a low cost shore protection device. Important factors in selecting a device will include the relative steepness of the offshore bottom slope, and whether a sand beach is present at the base of the bluff. These are often derived from bluff materials that have fallen from above, and they provide a buffer against normal wave action and may serve as a suitable foundation for various protective devices. During severe wave activity, however, waves can reach the bluff itself and erode or undercut the toe. Depending on the strength and characteristics of the bluff materials, this may cause the bluff to fail in a relatively short time.

The slope of the offshore bottom is also important. If the offshore slopes are steep, deep water is closer to shore, larger waves can reach the bluff, and maintenance of a protective beach is more difficult.

Conversely, flat offshore slopes inhibit heavy wave action at the bluff and provide for potentially better protective beaches.

Low Erodible Plains and Sand Beaches

These are the most common shoreforms throughout most areas of the United States. They are primarily composed of sands and gravels that gently rise from the water's edge and seldom attain a height of more than five to ten feet above the Stillwater level.

Figure 6 is a definition sketch of an idealized beach profile. Waves approach from offshore, finally breaking and surging up the foreshore. Above the foreshore, the profile flattens considerably to form a broad berm, which is not reached by normal wave activity. The beach berm will sometimes be backed by a low scarp leading to a second berm and eventually to a bluff or sand dune.

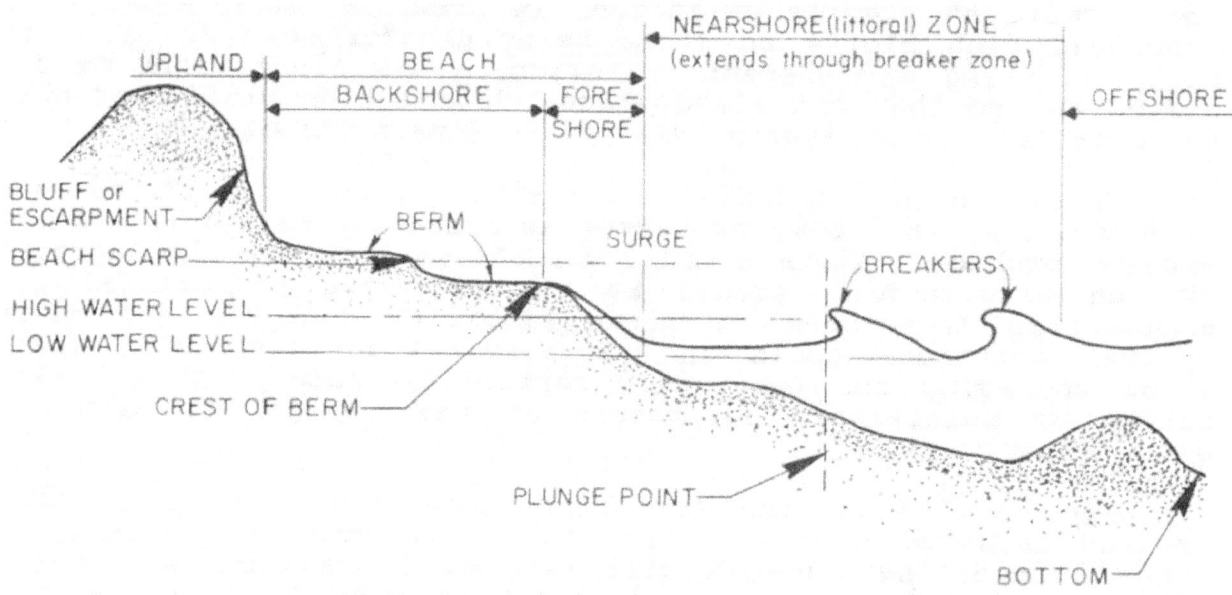

Figure 6   An Idealized Beach Profile
[After U.S. Army Corps of Engineers (1977c)]

The profile will reach some equilibrium shape in response to normal water levels and wave activity. This equilibrium will be disturbed and erosion will begin if the long-term water level rises or predominant wave heights increase. For a water level rise, a new equilibrium profile will eventually form with the same shape as the old, but shifted landward and upward. Similarly, increased wave activity causes a nearshore bar to grow as the beach erodes. Eventually, as this bar grows and the depths of water decrease, the larger waves will break farther offshore. This weakens their attacks on the beach and equilibrium is restored.

At open coast sites, the return to normal water levels and waves will initiate a healing process that may return the profile to essentially its initial position. This is because the flat swells tend to move sand back to the beach from the nearshore bar. At sheltered sites, however, these swells are not present, so the healing process never occurs, and storm-caused erosion losses tend to be permanent.

Changes in the sediment supply from updrift will also cause movement of the profile. A decrease in th6 supply will cause the beach to erode, and the profile will retreat landward, while still maintaining the same shape. Conversely, an increase in the supply will cause accretion and the profile will advance toward the water.

Wetlands and Marshes

Although they are treated separately in this section, wetlands and marshes usually occur in combination with sand beaches or low erodible plains. For federal regulatory purposes, wetlands are defined as:

> Those areas that are inundated or saturated by surface or groundwater at a frequency and duration sufficient to support, and under normal circumstances do support, a prevalence of vegetation typically adapted to life in saturated soil conditions. Wetlands generally include swamps, marshes, bogs, and similar areas. [U. S. Army Corps of Engineers (1977b)]

Marsh plants are primarily herbaceous (lack woody stems) and include grasses, sedges and rushes. The species present depend on location and whether the marsh is low (regularly flooded) or high (irregularly flooded).

Until recently, marshes were considered undesirable and regularly drained and filled for new development or agriculture. Their value has now been recognized as an important environmental resource, but they also protect the shore by absorbing the energy of approaching waves and trapping sediment that is being carried along by currents. These shore protection qualities are particularly important when the marsh fronts a sandy beach or other area where erosion is to be prevented. In that case, the marsh provides a front line of defense for the shore. While it may not provide full protection, it may, at least, partially dampen wave action and allow for less massive and costly backup protection.

THE CAUSES OF EROSION

Wave Action

Wave action is the most obvious cause of shoreline erosion.

Littoral Material Supply

Stable shorelines are in a state of dynamic equilibrium. Waves keep the littoral materials in constant motion in the downdrift direction, and the shoreline remains stable provided there is an equal supply of material from updrift. When the updrift supply is deficient, the shoreline erodes.

A substantial portion of the littoral material supplied to shorelines is the result of updrift erosion. If large amounts of the updrift shoreline are suddenly protected, material is lost to the littoral system. This decreases the supply to the downdrift shore, resulting in erosion problems unless that land is also protected.

Determining the longshore transport direction is sometimes necessary. This is usually a difficult task because it depends on wave directions that can vary considerably with the seasons. Summer winds (and waves) may be from one predominant direction, while winter storm winds may be from an entirely different quadrant. When the winds and waves change direction, the transport direction also changes (transport reversal).

The gross longshore transport rate is the quantity of sand (usually in cubic yards per year) that moves past a fixed point in either direction. The net longshore transport rate is the quantity that moves in the predominant direction minus the quantity that moves the other way. The net transport rate is specified by both quantity and direction (e.g., 10,000 cubic yards per year to the east).

Transport rates are important when considering accretion devices such as breakwaters and groins because it is necessary to judge the effects of device construction on the littoral system, particularly with respect to potential downdrift damages. A precise estimate will not usually be possible, but it may be feasible to examine similar structures or harbor works that have been constructed in the past for evidence of accretion over known periods of time. If nothing else, this should reveal the predominant transport direction and a crude measure of the possible transport rate. This should be an acceptable level of precision for small scale, low cost devices.

Slope Stability

Slope stability analysis is covered in standard geotechnical engineering textbooks [e.g., Lambe and Whitman (1969) and Winterkorn and Fang (1975)]. Major stability problems are most likely at high bluff shorelines where the heights are 20 feet or more. Except where toe protection is needed, slope stability problems on high bluffs tend to be beyond the range of low cost solutions.

A LOOK AT THE OPTIONS

Three basic choices are possible in response to an erosion problem: no action, relocation of endangered structures, and positive corrective measures. The latter includes devices that directly armor the shore, those that intercept and dissipate wave energy, and those that retain the earth slopes against sliding. Each alternative requires an evaluation of the planned land uses, money and time available, and other effects that may result from the decision.

NO ACTION

This is a decision-aid that can be used to evaluate different alternatives. Because even low cost solutions can require substantial investments, it is preferable to closely estimate potential losses using this alternative, particularly if no dwellings are directly threatened, and only undeveloped land or inexpensive structures are in danger. Also, erosion problems are sometimes caused by temporary factors (e.g., unusually high Great Lakes levels) that may abate. The resulting erosion, therefore, may slow before any action is taken. This could eliminate the immediate need for protective devices, or it could mean choosing a smaller scale, less expensive, device.

RELOCATION

In most cases, some action is necessary. It may be less expensive to relocate endangered structures than to invest in shore protection. Relocation can be to an entirely different site or it can be a setback farther from the water at the present site. The required setback must be carefully evaluated because the considerable expense of moving a building could be wasted if the setback is insufficient.

The first step is to evaluate the long-term erosion rate. This is difficult because reliable historical data on past shoreline positions is often lacking. Possible sources of data include a time sequence of aerial photographs or shoreline maps. If the property owner has occupied the site for many years (say 25 or more), and has observed slow shoreline retreat during that time, the annual erosion rate could be approximated by dividing the total amount of retreat by the number of years of observation. For instance, if the shoreline steadily receded 300 feet in 30 years, the estimated average erosion rate is about 10 feet/year. A setback of 100 feet could produce an additional 10 years of life for a structure, *provided erosion continues at* the *same rate.*

Conversely, if the shoreline was stable for years and suddenly retreated 300 feet in only 5 years, relocation on the same site may be risky and not generally advisable unless considerable setback room is available.

BULKHEADS AND SEAWALLS

The terms bulkhead and seawall are often used interchangeably. In a strict sense, however, bulkheads are retaining walls whose primary purpose is to hold or prevent sliding of the soil while providing protection from light-to-moderate wave action. Seawalls, on the other hand, are structures whose primary purpose is to protect the backshore from heavy wave action. Their massive size generally places them beyond the low cost range. Also, they are not generally needed in sheltered waters where large waves are not generated (except perhaps in the Great Lakes).

Bulkheads can be used to protect eroding bluff s by retaining soil at the toe, thereby increasing stability, or by protecting the toe from erosion and undercutting. They are also used for reclamation where a fill is needed in advance of the existing shore. Finally, bulkheads are used for marina and other structures, where deep water is needed directly at the shore (Figure 7).

Construction of a bulkhead does not insure stability of a bluff. If a bulkhead is placed at the toe of a high bluff steepened by erosion to the point of incipient failure, the bluff above the bulkhead may slide, burying or moving the structure toward the water. To increase the chances of success, the bulkhead should be placed lakeward of the bluff toe, and if possible, the bluff should be graded to a flatter, more stable slope.

Bulkheads protect only the land immediately behind them and offer no protection to adjacent areas up- or downcoast, or to the fronting beach. In fact, their vertical faces reflect wave energy, which may cause increased scour and could lead to a loss of any existing fronting beach. If the downdrift beaches were previously supplied by erosion of the land now protected, they may erode even more quickly. If a beach is to be maintained adjacent to a bulkhead, additional structures such groins or detached breakwaters may be required.

Bulkheads may be either cantilevers or anchored (like sheet piling), or gravity structures (like sand-filled bags). Cantilever bulkheads require adequate embedment to retain soil, and are used where low heights are sufficient. Toe scour reduces their effective embedment and can cause failure. Anchored bulkheads are usually used where higher structures are needed. They also require adequate embedment (although less than cantilever bulkheads) to function properly, but they tend to be less susceptible to toe scour.

Gravity structures eliminate the need for heavy pile driving equipment and are often appropriate where subsurface conditions hinder pile penetration. However, they require strong foundation soils to adequately support their weight, and they normally do not sufficiently penetrate the ground to develop reliable soil resistance on the offshore side. Therefore, they depend primarily on shearing resistance along the base of the bulkhead to support the applied loads. Gravity bulkheads also cannot prevent rotational slides in materials where the failure surface passes beneath the structure. Their use, therefore, is generally limited to relatively low heights where their cost is comparable to cantilever sheet pile bulkheads.

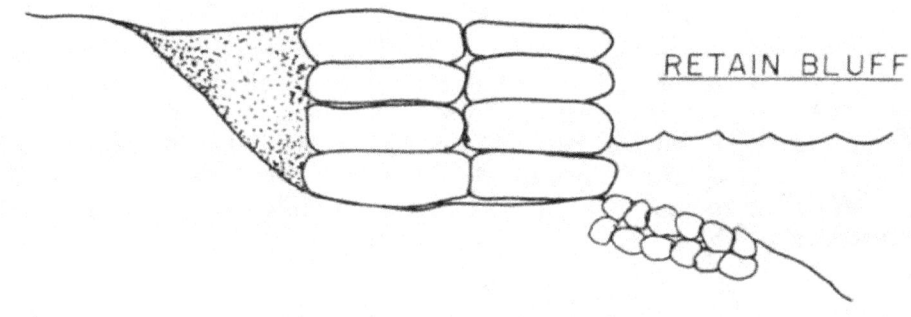

RETAIN BLUFF

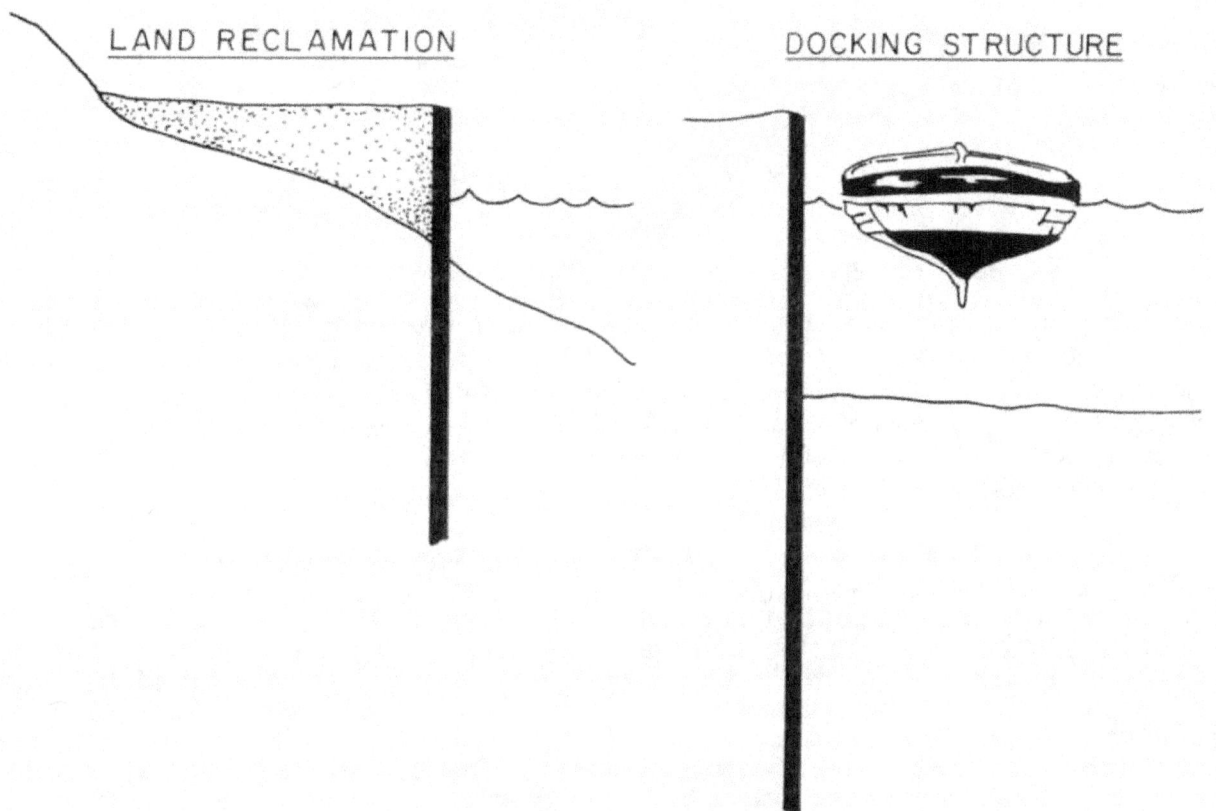

LAND RECLAMATION

DOCKING STRUCTURE

Figure 7   Uses of Bulkheads

REVETMENTS

A revetment is placed on a slope to protect it and adjacent uplands against scour (Figure 8). It depends on the underlying soil for support, so it must be built on a stable slope. An unstable bank must first be properly graded before construction. Fill material, when needed to achieve a uniform grade, must be adequately compacted.

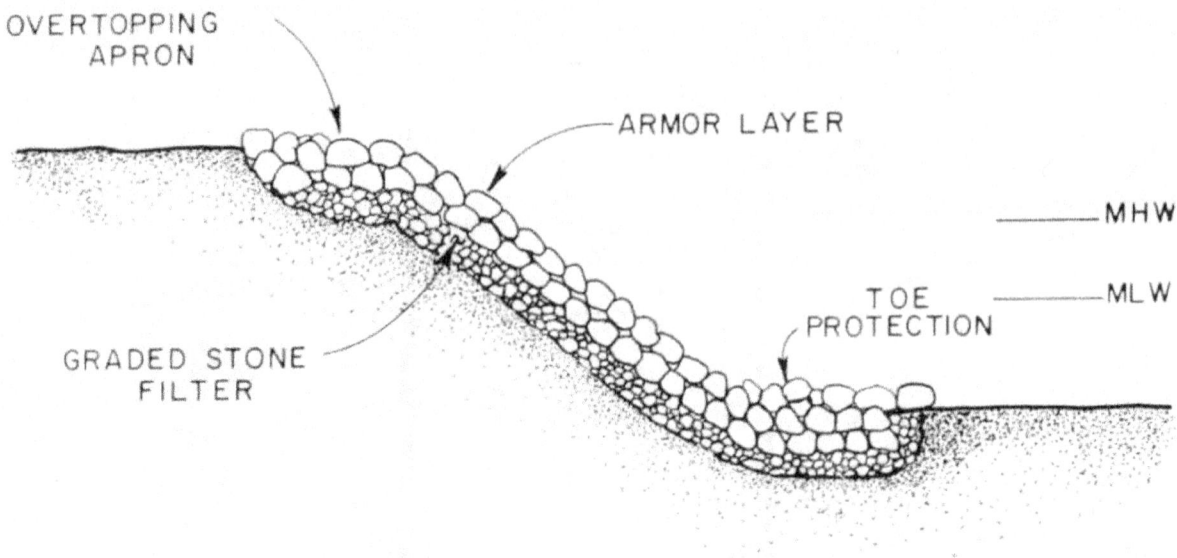

Figure 8   Typical Revetment Section

Revetments protect only the land immediately behind them and provide no protection to adjacent areas. Erosion may continue on adjacent shores, and near the revetment may be accelerated by wave reflection from the structure, although not as seriously as with vertical-faced bulkheads. Also, the downdrift shore may experience increased erosion if it was formerly supplied with material eroded from the now protected area. If a beach is to be maintained in front of a revetment, additional structures such as groins or detached breakwaters may be required.

A revetment consists of an armor layer, filter and toe. The armor must resist the waves, and settlement, and provides drainage of slope must be sufficiently flat to provide stability. Typical armor materials include quarrystone and various concrete blocks. The filter supports the armor groundwater through the revetment, and prevents the retained soil from being washed through the armor layer by waves or groundwater seepage. Toe protection prevents displacement of the seaward edge of the revetment.

Overtopping by green water (not white spray) may cause erosion at the top of the revetment. Problems from overtopping can be minimized by choosing a structure height that is greater than the expected runup height, or by providing an overtopping apron at the top of the revetment.

Flanking is another potential problem that can be prevented by tying each end of the revetment into adjacent shore protection structures or the existing bank. However, if the bank recedes, the ends will have to be periodically extended to maintain contact.

BREAKWATERS

Breakwaters are constructed offshore to dissipate the energy of approaching waves and form a protected shadow zone on their landward sides. (Figure 9). The ability of waves to transport sediment is a function of the wave height-squared, so a relatively modest decrease in incoming wave heights can have a major effect on sediment transport. For instance, if incoming waves are reduced to 70% of their original height after passing a breakwater, their ability to move sediment will decrease to 0.70 x 0.70 or 49% of their original capacity. Therefore, longshore-moving littoral drift will tend to accumulate behind the structure. The ability of a breakwater to trap sand is a function of its distance offshore, length parallel to shore, porosity, and spacing (where more than one breakwater is used).

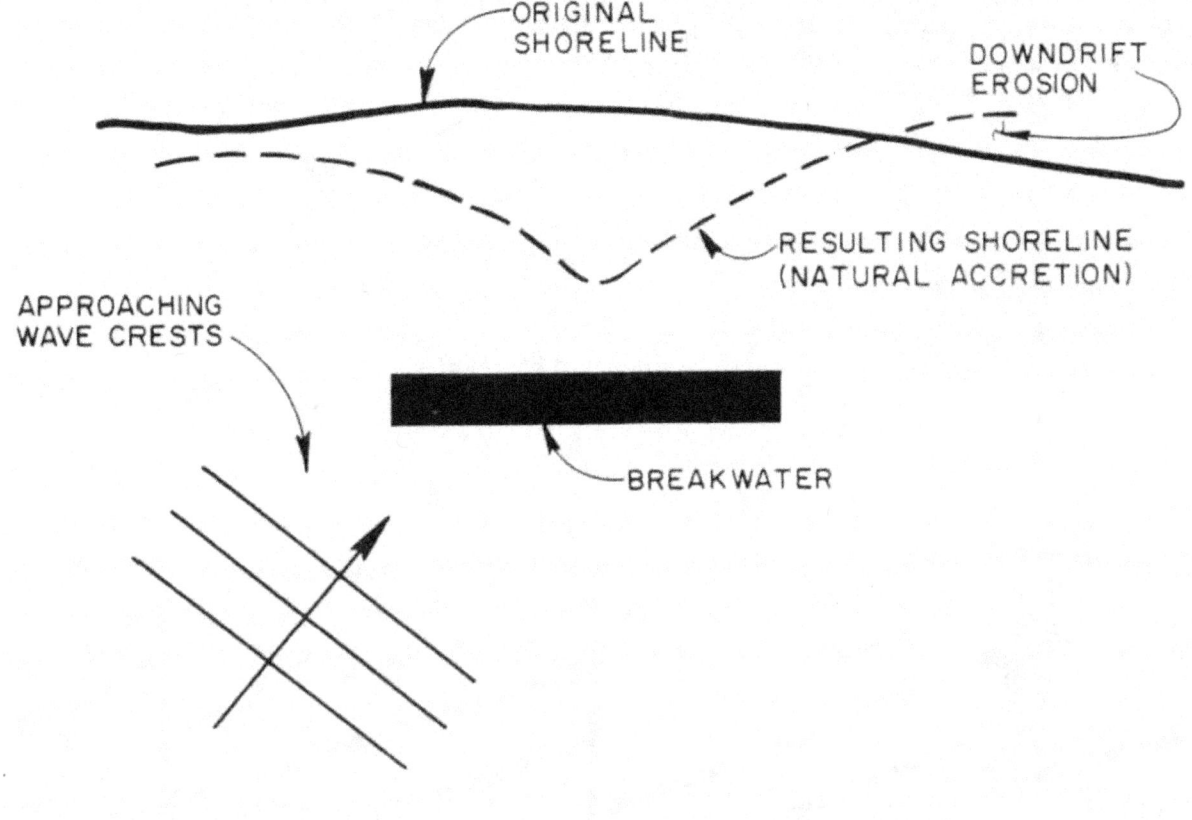

Figure 9   Plan View of a Breakwater

If accretion continues until the breakwater is joined to the shore, the resulting system would act as a large groin that would totally block the sand supply to the downdrift beach. This could cause significant erosion damages. Therefore, the area landward of the breakwater should be partially filled with sand after construction is completed. This may allow sand to continue past the structure and on to the downdrift beach without causing serious erosion problems.

Breakwaters are either fixed or floating. Fixed breakwaters are large masses of heavy material that rest on the bottom. Floating breakwaters are constructed of buoyant materials such as logs, hollow concrete boxes and scrap rubber tires. The latter are most popular because of their durability and ready, no-cost availability. Floating breakwaters are generally effective in sheltered waters where short-period (less than five seconds) waves are dissipated as they pass floating structures. Such waves have short lengths that may be less than the width of the breakwater.

GROINS

Groins are constructed perpendicular to shore and extend, finger-like, out into the water. Used singly or in groups known as groin fields, they trap sand or retard its longshore movement (Figure 10). Sand tends to accumulate on the updrift side of a groin while erosion occurs downdrift. This will cause the shoreline to rotate and align itself with the crests of the incoming waves, gradually decreasing the angle between the waves and the shore. In turn, the longshore transport rate will decrease and the shoreline will stabilize. The fillets of sand that collect on the updrift sides of the groins act as protective buffers. Storm waves attack these accumulations first, before reaching the unprotected backshore.

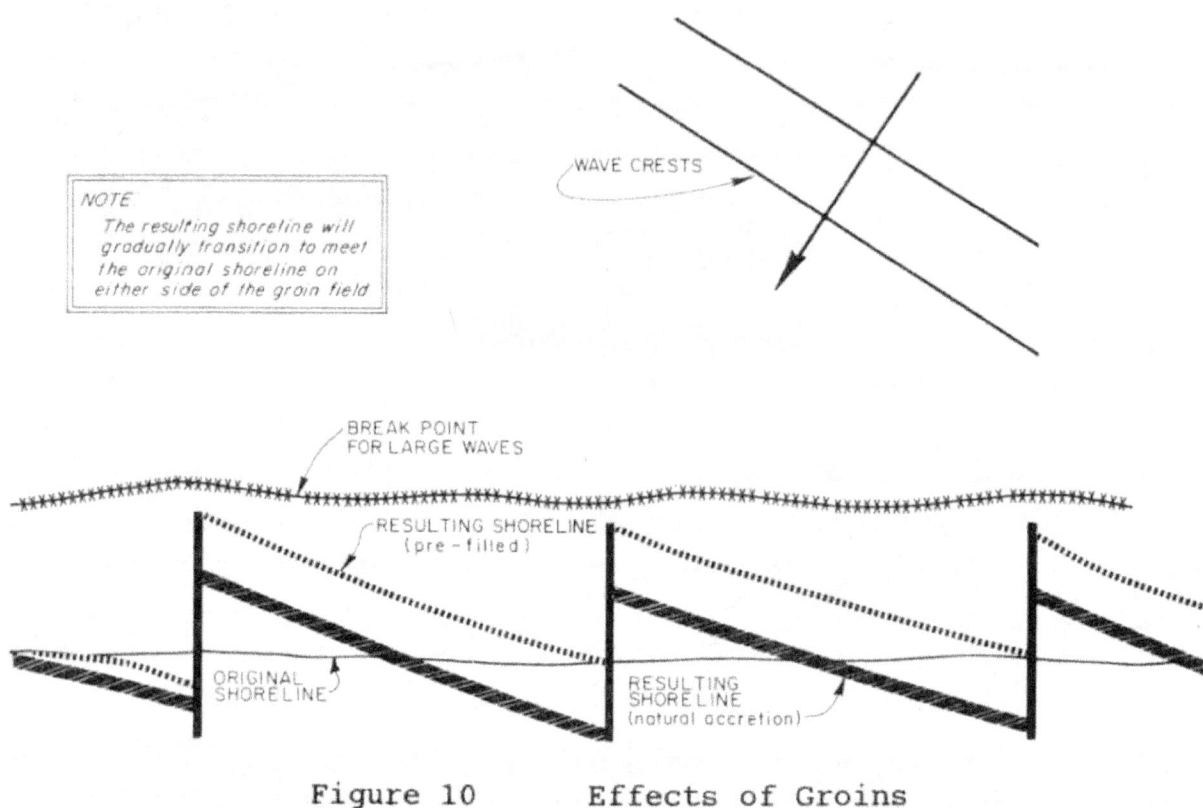

Figure 10   Effects of Groins

Without the sand fillets, groins cannot protect the shoreline from wave action, nor are they effective where the waves approach perpendicular to shore. Groin installations also require an adequate sand supply and are not effective where the littoral materials are finer than sand. Silts and clays tend to move in suspension and are not retained by groins on the beach.

When a groin is first built, the sand trapped on its updrift side is no longer available to downdrift beaches and erosion may result. When the updrift fillet is completely formed, the sand will pass around or over the groin to the downdrift shore, but at a slower rate than before it was built. If erosion of the downdrift shore is unacceptable (it usually is), an alternative is to build more than one groin and fill the area between with sand. This minimizes the downdrift damages and limits the erosion at the groin's shoreward end.

Groins can be built either high or low with respect to the existing beach profile. High groins effectively block the supply of sand to downdrift beaches, provided sand cannot pass through them. Low groins, built to be overtopped by waves either during storms or at a given tide level, permit sand to pass over them and nourish downdrift beaches.

A groin's length must be sufficient to create the desired beach shape while still allowing sand to pass around its outer end. If a groin extends seaward past the breaker zone, the sediment moving around the structure may be forced too far offshore to return to the adjacent downdrift beach. If it is too short, it may not trap enough sand to provide the desired beach.

The correct spacing of individual groins within a field is often difficult to determine and is a function of their length and the desired final shoreline shape. If groins are too far apart, excessive erosion can occur between them. If spaced too closely, they may not function properly. This is particularly true for long groins where sand passing around their ends must follow a curved path back to the beach. If the groins are too close together, the sand will be unable to reach the beach before it is again forced seaward by the next downdrift groin.

A groin must be built to resist wave forces, currents, the impact of floating debris, and earth pressures created by the difference in sand levels on both sides. As with other structures, groins must resist toe scour, and must be constructed to prevent failure due to flanking (erosion at their landward end).

BEACH FILLS

Beach fills are quantities of sand placed on the shoreline by mechanical means, such as dredging from offshore deposits or overland hauling by trucks. The resulting beach provides some protection to the area behind it and also serves as a valuable recreational resource.

The beach fill functions as an eroding buffer zone. Its useful life will depend on how quickly it erodes; a rapid succession of severe storms can completely eliminate a new fill in a short time. The owner must then be prepared to periodically renourish (add more fill) as erosion continues. Beach fills generally have relatively low initial costs but periodic maintenance costs needed for adding new fill.

VEGETATION

A planting program to establish desired species of vegetation is an inexpensive approach to shoreline protection and erosion control. Depending on where stabilization is desired, species from one of two general groups should be selected to insure adequate growth.

Found on parts of shorelines flooded periodically by brackish water, species of grasses, sedges, and rushes occur in marshes of moderate to low energy shorelines. Once extensive and widely distributed, marsh areas were viewed in the past as useless and were subjected to filling and diking. However, their destruction has lessened as their importance in the ecosystem and to shoreline protection has been realized.

Upland species (shrubs and trees but particularly grasses) are especially adapted to growing in the low-nutrient, low-moisture environment of the higher beach elevations, where they are subject to abrasion by windblown sand particles. Used to trap sand and stabilize the beach, upland vegetation also improves the beauty of a shoreline, prevents erosion during heavy rain, diminishes the velocity of overland flow, increases the soils infiltration rate, and provides a habitat for wildlife.

Even though vegetation provides significant help in stabilizing slopes and preventing erosion, vegetation alone cannot prevent erosion from heavy wave action or prevent movement of shoreline bluffs activated by groundwater action. In those instances, structural devices augmented with vegetation are recommended.

The effectiveness of vegetation is also limited by characteristics of the site. For instance, the site requirements which determine the effectiveness of a tidal marsh planting include: elevation and tidal regime, which determine the degree, duration, and timing of plant submergence; slope of the site; exposure to wave action; type of soil; salinity regime; and oxygen-aeration times. Plants which are specially adapted for higher beach elevations must tolerate rapid sand accumulation, flooding, salt spray, abrasion by wind-borne sand particles, wind and water erosion, wide temperature fluctuations, drought, and low nutrient levels. Appropriate species also vary with geographical location, climate, and distance from the water (vegetative zone).

INFILTRATION AND DRAINAGE CONTROLS

Infiltration and drainage controls are often needed to achieve stability along high bluff shorelines. Although many factors lead to slope stability problems, the presence of groundwater is one of the most important, since the majority of slope failures and landslides occur during or after periods of heavy rainfall or increased groundwater elevations. Infiltration controls prevent water from entering the ground, while drainage controls remove water that is already present in the soil.

Infiltration can be controlled by appropriate ditches and swales, and by sealing the ground surface. Surface cracks that develop when a slope begins to fail can be an easy path for water to enter, exert hydrostatic pressures, and lead to further instability. Such cracks should be promptly filled with compacted, relatively impermeable soil (preferably clay) to reduce the potential for such detrimental effects.

Drainage of the subsurface can be accomplished using vertical or horizontal drains. Standard design techniques and methods are described in civil engineering references such as Winterkorn and Fang (1975).

SLOPE FLATTENING

A bluff slope may be flattened to enhance its stability when adequate room exists, and there is no interference with the desired land use. Freshly excavated slopes should be planted to prevent erosion from surface runoff. It may also be necessary to build a revetment or bulkhead at the toe of the slope to protect against wave action.

PERCHED BEACHES

A perched beach (Figure 11) combines a low breakwater or sill and a beach fill perched, or elevated, above the normal level. This alternative provides a broad buffer against wave action while offering a potentially excellent recreational site. The sill can be constructed of various materials, but it must be impermeable to the passage of the retained beach sand by using, for instance, a filter cloth behind and beneath the structure. The cloth prevents the fill from escaping through any large voids in the sill and also stabilizes the structure against settlement. While a graded stone core could also be used in a rock sill in place of filter cloth, the limited height of such sills generally precludes use of muli-layered structures of this kind. The figure also shows a splash apron which is provided to prevent scour and erosion of the beach fill from overtopping waves.

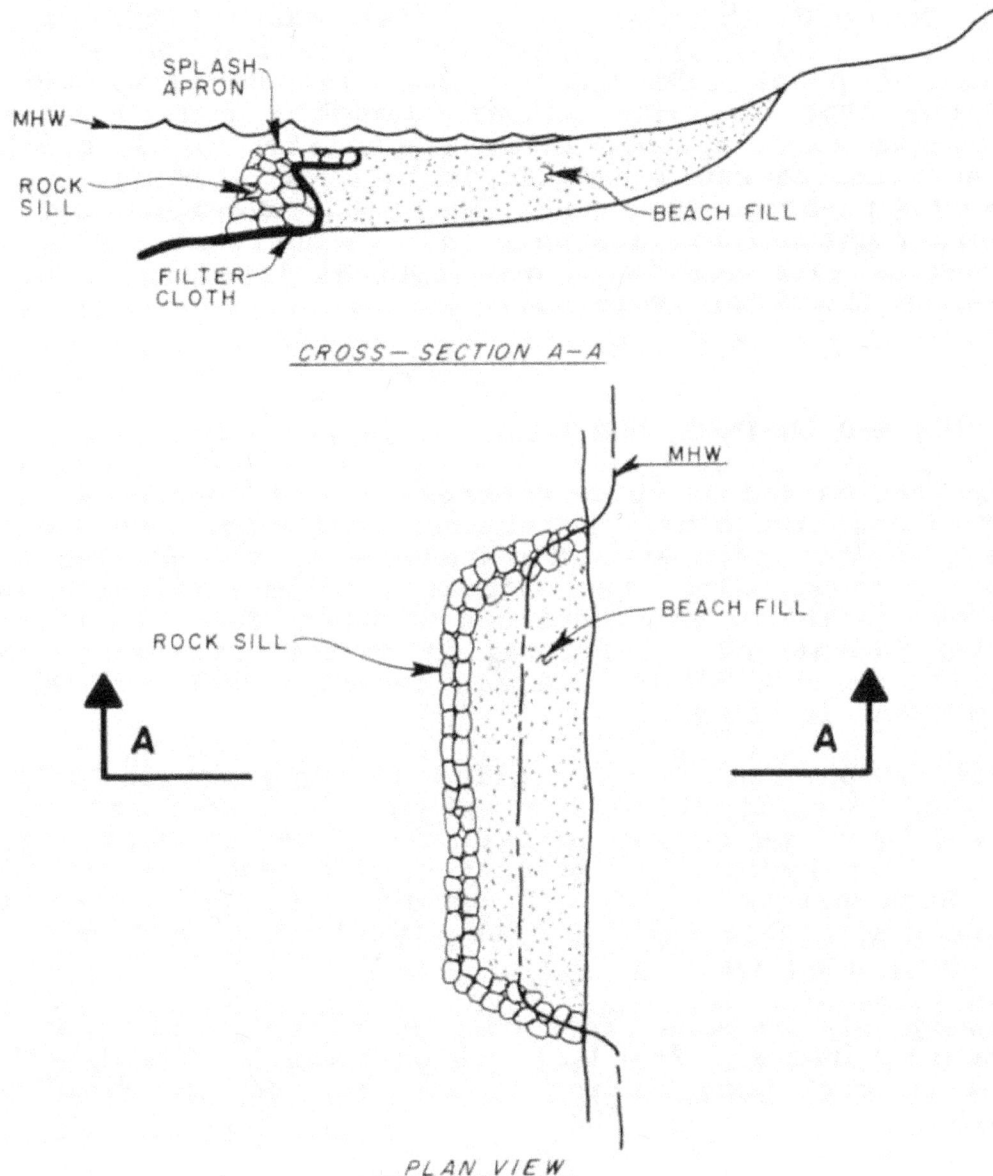

CROSS— SECTION A—A

PLAN VIEW

Figure 11   Perched Beach

Perched beaches can be provided where offshore slopes are mild enough to permit the use of a sill in shallow water at a reasonable distance from shore.

STRUCTURES AND FILLS

In addition to perched beaches, fills can also be incorporated in groin systems and with breakwaters. In fact, auxiliary fills are almost mandatory in most cases, otherwise serious erosion problems can occur downdrift.

STRUCTURES AND VEGETATION

While vegetation is one means of controlling shoreline erosion, its most serious deficiency is its restriction to areas of limited fetch because it cannot become established in heavy wave environments. Vegetation can be used in areas experiencing considerably heavier wave activity, however, if it is placed in the shadow of a structure such as a breakwater. The use of temporary structures is particularly appealing because they provide protection while the plants need it, and can then be removed later when the plantings have matured.

THE DESIGN PROBLEM

FUNCTIONAL DESIGN

Shoreform Compatibility

Certain approaches are better suited to particular shoreline configurations than others. It is important to choose a method appropriate to the dominant shoreform at the site.

Bluff Shorelines. The *no action* alternative can be appropriate for bluffs since it does not disrupt natural shoreline processes and requires no investment for protective structures. Eventually, however, the property may be totally destroyed by erosion. While relocation does not disrupt shoreline processes, and it can permanently eliminate any threat to buildings, it can cost as much as or more than a protective structure. *Bulkheads* are ideally suited, either for full-height retention of low bluffs, or as toe protection for high bluffs. Constructed of readily available materials and easily repaired if damaged, they are particularly useful where offshore slopes are steep. They can, however, induce toe scour and loss of beach material. Revetments are marginally effective in bluff situations. Low bluffs that can be flattened to a stable slope may be effectively protected by revetments, but high bluffs generally cannot be regraded. Revetments can protect the toes of high bluffs, either alone, or in conjunction with another device. *Breakwaters* reduce wave energy reaching the bluff but do not provide positive toe protection. They may build or maintain a beach (if an adequate sand supply exists), which provides some protection against normal waves, but would be ineffective against storm waves. Use of breakwaters generally requires gentle offshore slopes. *Groins* protect only to the extent they can build or hold a beach. Since they require a sand supply, they would not work in an area of clay or silt bluffs unless sand was imported. *Beach fills* provide some protection against normal wave action but would be ineffective during storms. Vegetation would provide little protection until well established and even then, does not positively protect against large storm waves. *Drainage controls* are mandatory if groundwater adversely affects slope stability. However, they provide no toe protection and can be expensive. *Slope flattening* provides a permanent solution for slope stability problems, but does not protect against continued wave action. It also requires adequate room at the top of the bluff for the slope. A *perched beach* would protect against normal waves but would be ineffective during storms. A *combination approach* can be the best solution. For instance, drainage controls should be used as needed, possibly with slope flattening. Toe protection could be provided with a revetment and a fronting sand beach to provide additional protection (provided offshore slopes are mild). Vegetation planted on the regraded slope would prevent erosion from runoff, and other species could be used to stabilize the beach fill.

Sand Beaches. The no action and relocation alternatives are applicable as they were for bluffs. *Bulkheads* are generally inappropriate unless an elevated feature, such as a promenade or parking lot, is needed. Vertical bulkheads induce toe scour and wave reflections, and could cause erosion of the beach fronting the bulkhead. Revetments are better for protecting features directly behind the beach since they absorb wave energy better and are more flexible when settlement occurs. They have an adverse aesthetic effect on the beach, however, and they can limit use or access to the shore. Use of revetments by a single landowner is often a problem because they are subject to flanking. *Breakwaters* are also well suited because they trap and hold sand moving along, on or offshore. They can cause extensive downdrift damages, however, because the trapped sand cannot reach adjacent beaches. They are also expensive to build. *Groins* can effectively build beaches on their updrift sides but can also cause accelerated downdrift erosion. Their functional behavior is complex and difficult to predict. *Beach fills* retain the natural form and character of the beach and enhance its recreational potential. Local sources of suitable sand are not always available, however, and fills require periodic renourishment. Vegetation, effective in many sheltered areas, has low initial costs and enhances the natural appearance and beauty of the shoreline. Unfortunately, foot and vehicular traffic damage plantings. *Drainage controls* and *slope flattening* are not applicable. *Perched beaches* can be used in some areas where fills alone would be too large to be economical, or where larger wave action is a problem. *Combination approaches* are often excellent, such as a perched beach that is further stabilized by vegetation.

Wetlands. Structures built near wetlands are usually placed at a low bluff or beach behind the marsh. For protection of the marsh itself, vegetation is the only appropriate alternative. To assist in establishing plantings, however, small temporary break*waters* may be required. *Beach fills or perched beaches* may also be used to provide a suitable substrate for planting in some areas.

Applicability to Shoreline Uses

Some methods lend themselves more readily than others to particular shoreline uses. It is important to choose a method that performs its function and does not interfere with the planned use of the shoreline. *No action* obviously does not enhance shoreline uses, although continued erosion may have an adverse impact. Relocation involves similar considerations. Bulkheads create an access problem unless stairs are provided. Vertical structures may also cause wave reflections that can erode the remaining beach material. Bulkheads are necessary when some water depth for boating activities is needed at the shore. *Revetments* of randomly placed rough stone may hinder access to the beach. Smooth structures, such as concrete blocks, cause less difficulty for walkers. Breakwaters provide an area sheltered from waves, but they can hinder circulation and cause water quality problems. Beaches built behind breakwaters have enhanced recreational potential. Rough stone structures may provide an improved habitat for certain fish species but may be hazardous to climbers. High structures may also intrude on the view of the water and be aesthetically undesirable. *Groins* may hinder travel along the beach, but any sand they trap improves the beach conditions. *Beach fills* enhance recreational uses of 'the shore, but increased turbidity during construction can temporarily harm certain fin and shellfish species. Vegetation greatly improves the natural habitat but hinders other uses of the beach because traffic through the plantings must be restricted. *Drainage controls* have little impact on shoreline uses and slope flattening reduces the available land at the shore. *Perched beaches* provide a recreational beach. A vertical sill may pose a hazard to bathers because of the sudden step to deeper water, but it may provide improved access for fishing. A rock sill may provide a natural habitat for fin and shellfish and may not be as hazardous to bathers.

Conditions in the General Area

Conditions in the local area can strongly influence the selection of an alternative. One of the most important considerations is the possible effects on downdrift properties. Accretion devices (breakwaters and groins) trap sand moving along the beach and tend to starve the downdrift shoreline. If this would cause damages to neighboring properties, the area behind the breakwater or updrift from the groin must be partially filled so that littoral material bypasses the structure, and downdrift damages are avoided.

Shoreline composition is also important. Accretion devices do not function in areas where little sand is in transit because they do not sufficiently calm the water to permit settlement of silts and clays. Slopes and soil composition are also important for determining appropriate plant species.

Finally, climatic and other environmental conditions must be considered. Plant species obviously must be planted where the climate permits survival and growth. salinity is critical for many species which can only tolerate changes of salinity within a narrow band. Warm salt water more easily corrodes steel and other metals than cold fresh water. Warm salt water is also the habitat of marine borers that attack submerged timber structures. On the other hand, fresh water lakes freeze in the winter, subjecting structures to large forces and abrasion from ice sheets. In some areas this may require more sturdy construction than would be required for resisting wave action at the site.

Summary

The factors relating each available alternative to shoreform and shoreline use are summarized on Tables 1 and 2.

Table 1

METHODS APPLICABLE TO VARIOUS SHOREFORMS

Alternative*	High Bluffs	Low Bluffs	Beaches	Wetlands
Relocation	Sometimes	Sometimes	Sometimes	Sometimes
Bulkheads	Usually	Almost always	Sometimes	Rarely
Revetments	Sometimes	Almost always	Almost always	Rarely
Breakwaters	Rarely	Rarely	Almost always	Sometimes
Groins	Almost never	Almost never	Almost always	Almost never
Beach Fills	Almost never	Almost never	Almost always	Rarely
Vegetation	Almost never	Almost never	sometimes	Almost always
Infiltration and Drainage Controls	Almost always	Usually	Almost never	Almost never
Slope Flattening	Rarely	Usually	Almost never	Almost never
Perched Beaches	Rarely	Rarely	Almost always	sometimes

* Applicability is for the alternative used alone in the given situation. Combination devices are not included.

Table 2

COMPATIBILITY OF ALTERNATIVES WITH SHORELINE USES

Alternative	Strolling	Bathing	Fishing	Boating
No Action	Sometimes	Sometimes	Usually	Usually
Relocation	Sometimes	Sometimes	Sometimes	Sometimes
Bulkheads	Usually	Sometimes	Almost always	Almost always
Revetments	Usually	Sometimes	Usually	usually
Breakwaters	Almost always	Almost always	Almost always	Usually
Groins	Usually	Almost always	Almost always	Usually
Beach Fills	Almost always	Almost always	Usually	Almost always
Vegetation	Almost never	Almost never	Almost always	Rarely
Infiltration and Drainage Controls	Almost always	Almost always	Almost always	Almost always
Slope Flattening	Almost always	Almost always	Almost always	Almost always
Perched Beaches	Almost always	Almost always	Almost always	Usually

STRUCTURAL DESIGN

If the chosen alternative involves construction of a physical shore protection device, several key problems must be resolved before an adequate structural design is completed. The first step is an evaluation of the potential water level and design wave height at the site. Other considerations include toe protection, filtering, flank protection, structure height, and various environmental factors.

Water Levels

A design water level must be determined before the wave height used to design structures can be found. In tidal waters, the elevation of the mean spring or diurnal tide is a sufficient starting point for low cost protection. Table 3 is reproduced from Tide Tables published by the National Ocean Survey (See Water level in the *OTHER HELP* Section). For instance, at Station 2037, Oxford, Maryland, the mean tide range is 1.4 feet, the spring range is 1. 6 feet, and the mean tide level is +O. 7 feet above chart datum (MLW). The average spring tide, therefore, is +1.5 feet above MLW (Figure 12). An   increment should be added to account for storm setup effects. Local experience should dictate, but values of two or three feet are probably reasonable for storm setup.

Attention should be drawn to the use of Mean Low Water (MLW) as datum in the previous discussion. This has been the datum used by the National Ocean Survey in the past for east coast navigation charts. In the future, however, the NOS will begin to adopt Mean Lower Low Water (MLLW) as datum for all nautical charts in the United States. This change will occur gradually as charts are periodically revised and reissued.

On the Great Lakes, the Monthly Bulletin of Lake Levels for the Great Lakes (see Water Levels in the *Other Help* Section) summaries of water levels for the previous year and the current year to date, as well as projected lake levels for the next six months. For each lake, a curve is also given for the long-term average lake level (1900 to the present) (See Figure 13). A suggested design water level is the greater of (a) the water level midway between the long-term average and the recorded maximum average monthly water level or (b) the highest monthly water level that has occurred during the preceding year. For instance, on Lake Michigan, the highest average water levels occur in July when they are about 2.0 feet above chart datum (576.8 feet). (Low Water Datum (LWD) is +576.8 feet IGLD for Lake Michigan.) The maximum observed monthly water level for July on Lake Michigan was observed in 1974 at +4.2 feet. A water level midway between them is +3.1 feet. The maximum observed monthly water level during the previous year was +3.0 feet, so the chosen water level should be the greater of the two or +3.1 feet (579.9 feet).

Storm setup or seiche values should be added to obtain a final water level. Figure 14 contains suggested values from Help Yourself [U. S. Army Corps of Engineers (1978d)] superimposed on a map of the Great Lakes - The design lake level, therefore, will be the sum of the lake level found in the previous step and the storm setup value.

Wave Heights

Waves at a site are generated either by wind action or moving vessels. At most locations, however, wind action is more critical for design. The design wave will be the lesser of (a) the maximum height generated by wind acting along the critical fetch or (b) the maximum breaker height that can reach the site during design water level conditions. In other words, if the wind can produce a larger wave than can be supported at the site, the available depth will control, not the wind.

No.	PLACE	POSITION Lat.	Long.	DIFFERENCES Time High water	Low water	Height High water	Low water	RANGES Mean	Spring	Mean Tide Level
		° ' N.	° ' W.	h. m.	h. m.	feet	feet	feet	feet	feet
	VIRGINIA — Continued Chesapeake Bay, Eastern Shore — Con. *Time meridian, 75°W.*			on HAMPTON ROADS, p.88						
1959	Occohannock Creek-------------	37 33	75 55	+2 02	+2 32	-0.8	0.0	1.7	2.0	0.9
1961	Pungoteague Creek-------------	37 40	75 50	+2 22	+2 37	-0.8	0.0	1.7	2.0	0.8
1963	Onancock, Onancock Creek------	37 43	75 45	+2 52	+3 09	-0.7	0.0	1.8	2.2	0.9
1965	Watts Island-----------------	37 48	75 54	+2 59	+3 02	-0.9	0.0	1.6	1.9	0.8
1967	Tangier Sound Light----------	37 47	75 58	+2 51	+2 48	*0.64	*0.64	1.6	1.9	0.8
1969	Muddy Creek Entrance---------	37 51	75 40	+3 14	+3 43	-0.3	0.0	2.2	2.6	1.1
	MARYLAND Chesapeake Bay, Eastern Shore									
1971	Ape Hole Creek, Pocomoke Sound------	37 58	75 49	+3 24	+3 48	-0.2	0.0	2.3	2.8	1.1
	Pocomoke River									
1973	Shelltown-------------------	37 59	75 38	+3 29	+4 06	-0.1	0.0	2.4	2.9	1.2
1975	Pocomoke City--------------	38 05	75 34	+5 46	+6 05	-0.9	0.0	1.6	2.0	0.8
1976	Snow Hill, city park-------	38 10	75 24	+7 32	+7 43	-0.6	0.0	1.9	2.3	1.0
1977	Janes Island Light----------	37 58	75 55	+3 51	+3 50	-0.7	0.0	1.8	2.2	0.9
1979	Crisfield, Little Annemessex River--	37 59	75 52	+3 47	+3 55	-0.5	0.0	2.0	2.4	1.0
1981	Long Point, Big Annemessex River----	38 03	75 48	+4 16	+4 36	-0.4	0.0	2.1	2.5	1.0
1983	Teague Creek, Manokin River--------	38 06	75 50	+4 35	+4 55	-0.4	0.0	2.1	2.5	1.0
1985	Ewell, Smith Island--------------	38 00	76 02	+3 56	+4 21	*0.64	*0.64	1.6	1.9	0.8
1987	Solomons Lump Light-------------	38 03	76 01	+4 13	+4 15	-0.8	0.0	1.7	2.0	0.8
1989	Holland Island Bar Light--------	38 04	76 06	+4 13	+4 20	*0.56	*0.56	1.4	1.7	0.7
1991	Sharkfin Shoal Light------------	38 12	75 59	+4 43	+4 56	-0.3	0.0	2.2	2.6	1.1
1993	Great Shoals Light, Monie Bay-------	38 13	75 53	+4 57	+5 12	-0.2	0.0	2.3	2.8	1.2
	Wicomico River									
1995	Whitehaven-----------------	38 16	75 47	+5 24	+5 37	-0.1	0.0	2.4	2.9	1.2
1997	Salisbury-----------------	38 22	75 36	+6 18	+6 14	+0.5	0.0	3.0	3.6	1.5
	Nanticoke River									
1999	Roaring Point-------------	38 16	75 55	+4 57	+5 25	-0.2	0.0	2.3	2.8	1.2
2001	Vienna--------------------	38 29	75 49	+7 30	+7 36	-0.2	0.0	2.3	2.8	1.2
2003	Sharptown----------------	38 32	75 43	+8 16	+8 18	0.0	0.0	2.5	3.0	1.3
2005	Fishing Point, Fishing Bay----------	38 18	76 01	+5 01	+5 24	0.0	0.0	2.5	3.0	1.2
2007	Hooper Strait Light---------------	38 14	76 05	+4 52	+4 57	-0.8	0.0	1.7	2.0	0.8
				on BALTIMORE, p.80						
2009	Hooper Island Light---------------	38 15	76 15	-5 07	-5 23	+0.4	0.0	1.5	1.8	0.7
2011	Barren Island---------------------	38 20	76 16	-4 52	-5 07	+0.2	0.0	1.3	1.5	0.6
	Little Choptank River									
2013	Taylors Island, Slaughter Creek-	38 28	76 18	-3 27	-3 14	+0.2	0.0	1.3	1.5	0.6
2015	Woolford, Church Creek----------	38 30	76 10	-3 25	-3 10	+0.3	0.0	1.4	1.6	0.7
2017	Cherry Island, Beckwiths Creek--	38 34	76 13	-3 21	-3 11	+0.2	0.0	1.3	1.5	0.6
2019	Hudson Creek-------------------	38 35	76 15	-3 49	-3 31	+0.3	0.0	1.4	1.6	0.7
2021	Sharps Island Light--------------	38 38	76 23	-3 51	-4 00	+0.2	0.0	1.3	1.5	0.6
	Choptank River									
2023	Choptank River Light-----------	38 39	76 11	-3 17	-3 18	+0.3	0.0	1.4	1.6	0.7
2025	Cambridge---------------------	38 34	76 04	-2 54	-2 50	+0.5	0.0	1.6	1.8	0.8
2027	Choptank---------------------	38 41	75 57	-2 13	-1 58	+0.5	0.0	1.6	1.8	0.8
2029	Dover Bridge-----------------	38 45	76 00	-0 57	-0 56	+0.6	0.0	1.7	2.0	0.8
2031	Denton-----------------------	38 53	75 50	+0 13	+0 22	+1.1	0.0	2.2	2.5	1.1
2033	Greensboro-------------------	38 58	75 49	+1 18	+1 08	+1.4	0.0	2.5	2.9	1.2
2035	Wayman Wharf, Tuckahoe Creek-----	38 53	75 57	+0 53	+0 25	+1.3	0.0	2.4	2.8	1.2
	Tred Avon River									
2037	Oxford-----------------------	38 42	76 10	-3 05	-3 00	+0.3	0.0	1.4	1.6	0.7
2039	Easton Point-----------------	38 46	76 06	-2 59	-2 50	+0.5	0.0	1.6	1.8	0.8
2041	Deep Neck Point, Broad Creek--------	38 44	76 14	-3 10	-3 01	+0.3	0.0	1.4	1.6	0.7
2043	St. Michaels, San Domingo Creek-----	38 46	76 14	-3 06	-3 06	+0.3	0.0	1.4	1.6	0.7
2045	Avalon, Dogwood Harbor----------	38 42	76 20	-3 08	-3 03	+0.2	0.0	1.3	1.5	0.6
2047	Poplar Island-----------------	38 46	76 23	-3 12	-3 18	+0.1	0.0	1.2	1.3	0.6
2049	Ferry Cove, Eastern Bay--------	38 46	76 20	-3 01	-3 04	-0.1	0.0	1.0	1.2	0.5

Table 3   Sample Tide Table
[U.S. Department of Commerce (1976)]

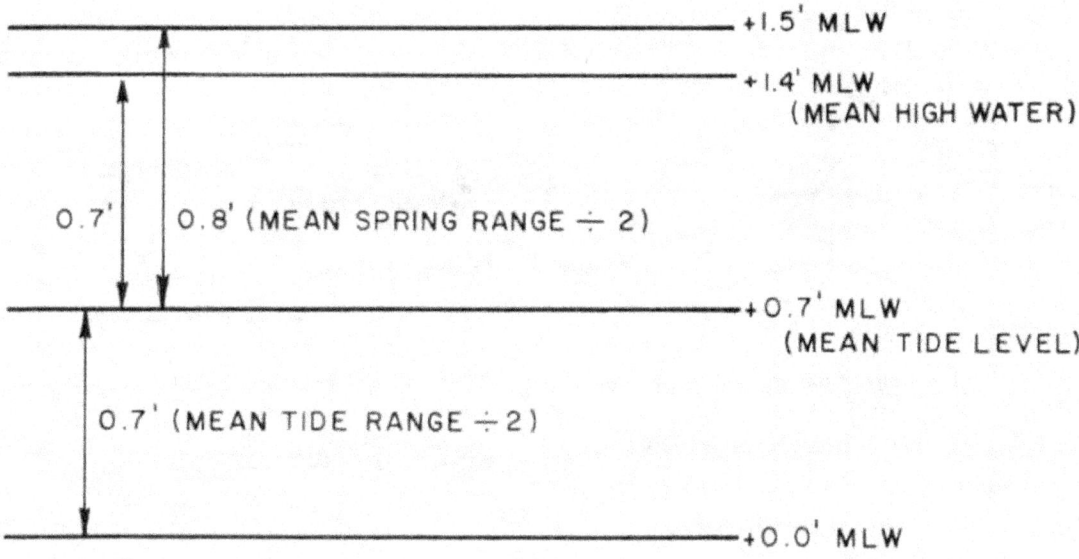

Figure 12   Reference Water Levels at Oxford, Maryland

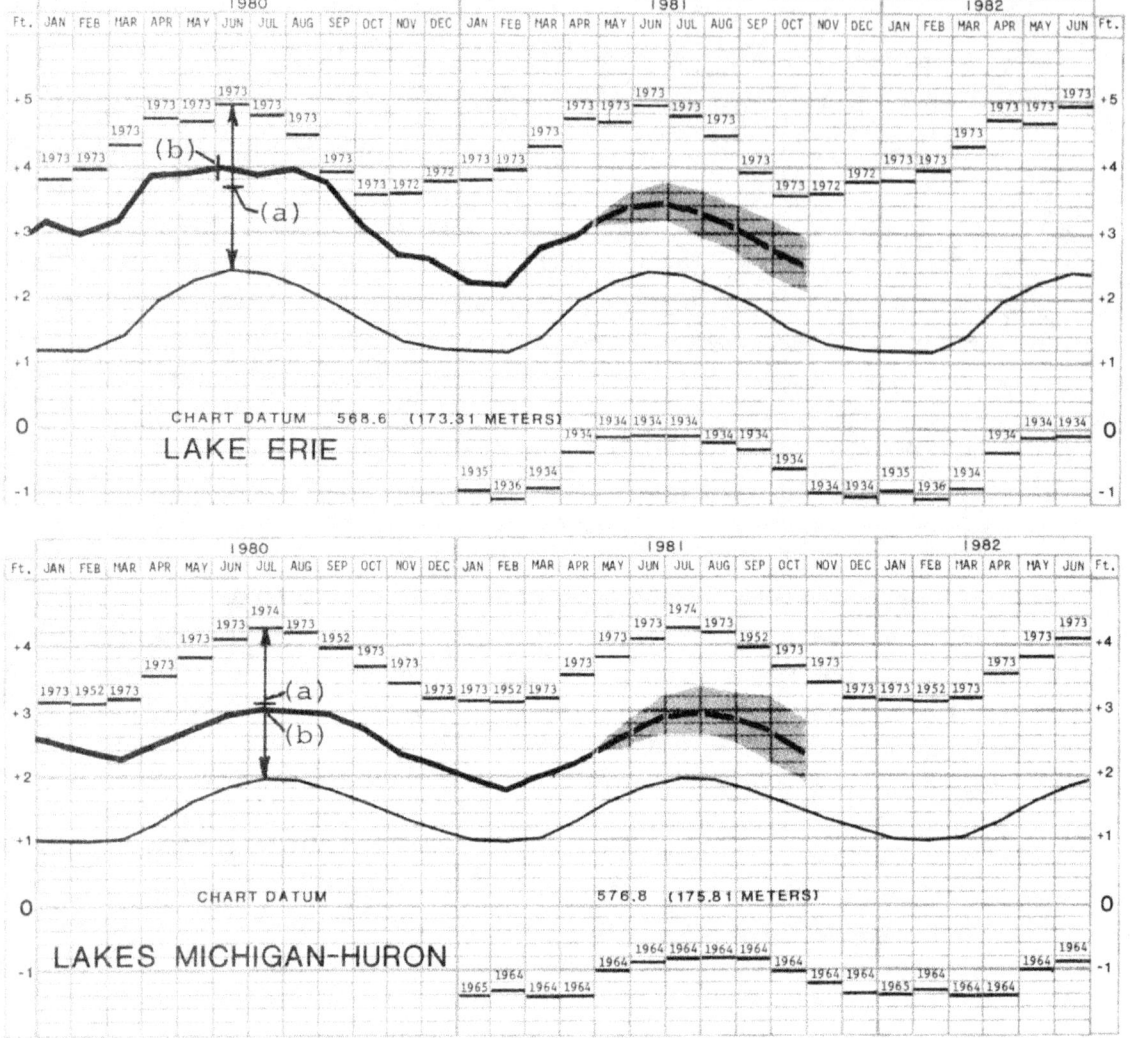

EXAMPLE
CHOOSE GREATER OF:

(a) Midway between long term average (Thin Line) and highest recorded monthly level. These are points (a)

(b) Highest water level recorded in previous 12 months (Thick Line). These are points (b).

LEGEND

▬▬▬ Actual monthly water levels for past 15 months
■ ■ ■ Projected monthly water levels for next 6 months
——— Average monthly water levels; 1900 to present
(DATE) Extreme monthly high and low water levels

Figure 13   Design Lake Levels
[After U.S. Army Corps of Engineers (1981a)]

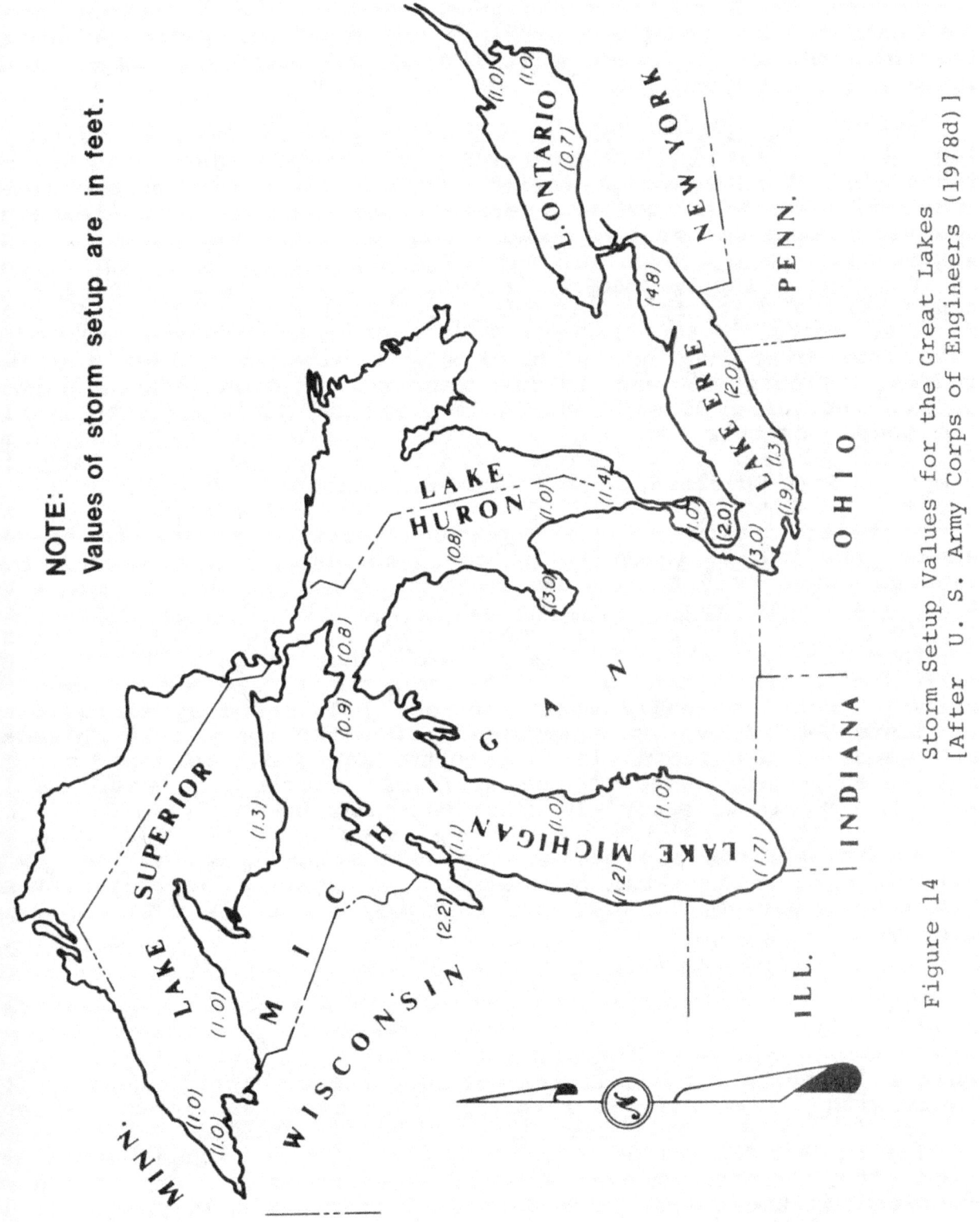

Figure 14   Storm Setup Values for the Great Lakes
[After U. S. Army Corps of Engineers (1978d)]

The height of wind-driven waves depends on several factors: wind speed, duration, fetch length and depth. When considering wind speed, it is important to realize that there must be sustained wind action to effectively generate waves. Brief gusts reaching high velocities do not last long enough to cause wave growth. The fastest-mile is a convenient way to characterize both wind speed and duration. The maximum fastest-mile is the highest speed that occurs with a sufficient duration for the wind to travel one mile. In other words, a 60-mile/hour wind must last for one minute to travel one mile, whereas a 30-mile/hour wind must last for two minutes. Figures 15 and 16 are maps of the continental United States, including Alaska, which displays the maximum fastest-mile wind speed contours for 10- and 25-year return periods. For example, the 10-year fastest-mile wind speed at New York City is 60 mph, and at Charleston, South Carolina it is 75 mph.

A brief review of the concept of return period is needed because the public tends to be confused about its meaning. For instance, when told that a device will withstand the 10-year wave at a site, most people will probably conclude that the structure will be safe for the next ten years. Or, if design wave conditions have occurred recently, they may assume that these will not occur again for another ten years. Neither of these perceptions is correct. What is really meant can be illustrated by an example. For instance, if over a long time (e.g., 100 years), 10 episodes with waves of a certain size were observed, the return period for that wave height, based on the available statistics, would be 10 years (100 years of record/10 observed episodes).

Return periods can be used to assess the risk involved in a particular decision. The probability, P, that a particular event with return period, T_r, will occur during a period of time, I , is given by,

$$P = [1 - (1 - 1/T_r)^I] * 100 \qquad (4)$$

Table 4 contains probabilities of occurrence (percentages) for events with 10- or 25-year return periods as a function of various project durations. For example, consider an individual who wishes to protect his shoreline for 10 years. Using methods explained later, the designer chooses a 10-year design wave. The chance of experiencing the design wave during a structure's 10-year life is 65 percent. If this is an unacceptable level of risk, the designer may then provide protection against a larger design wave, say 25 years. In that case, there is a 34-percent chance of the 25-year wave occurring during the structure's 10-year life. If this is an acceptable level of risk, the design can proceed on that basis.

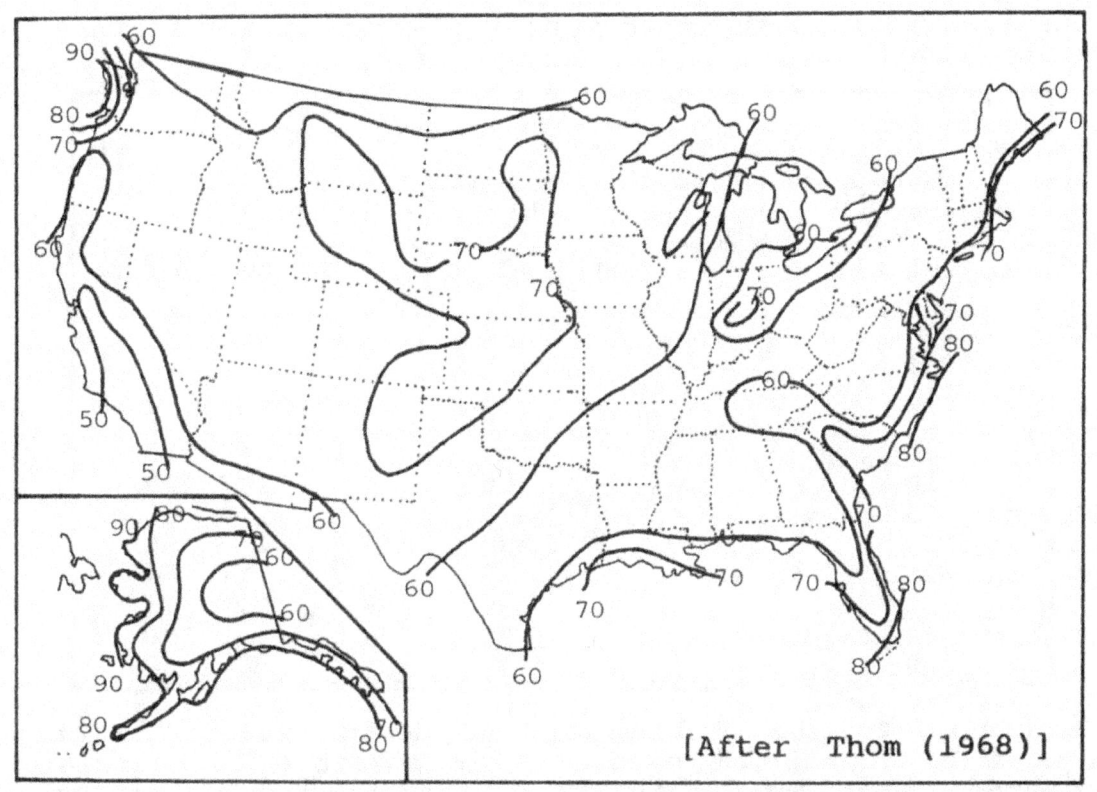

Figure 15   Fastest-Mile Wind Speeds: 10-year Return Period

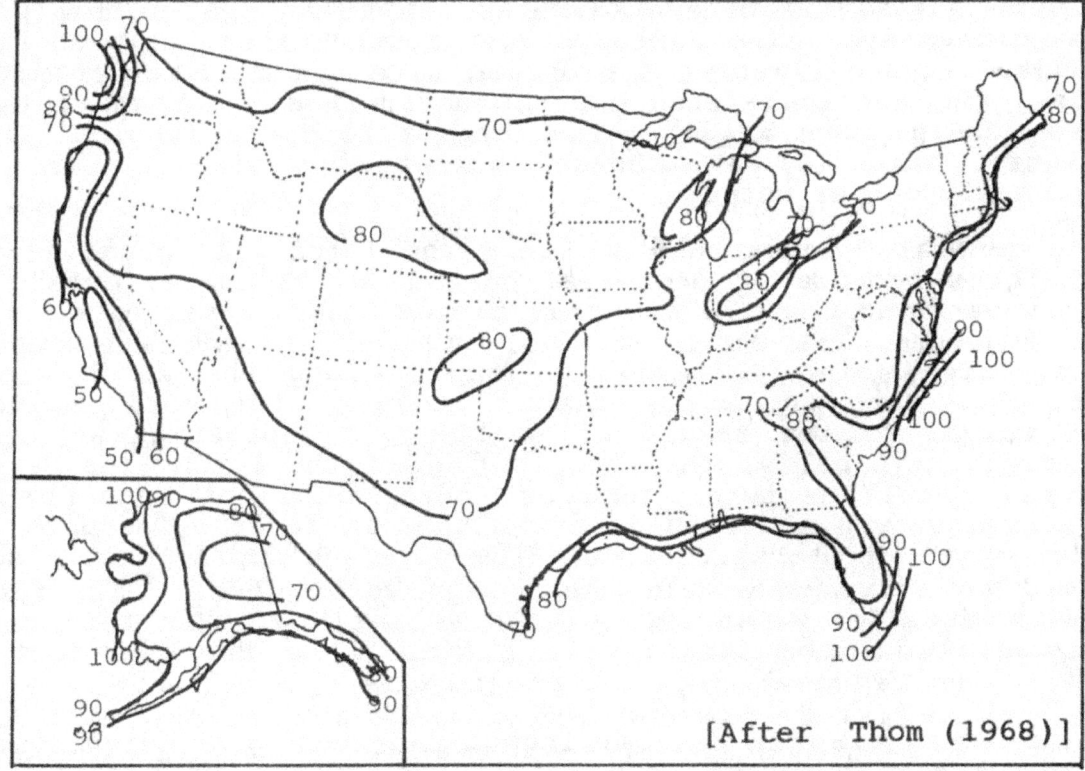

Figure 16   Fastest-Mile Wind Speeds: 25-year Return Period

Table 4

PERCENT CHANCE OF DESIGN EVENT OCCURRENCE

Project Life (years)	Design Condition Return Period (years)	
	10	25
1	10	4
2	19	8
5	41	18
10	65	34
15	79	46
20	88	56
25	93	64
30	96	71
40	99	80
50	99	87

Returning to the problem of the design wave, the critical fetch must be identified before it is possible to calculate the wave height. Fetch length is the distance across water that wind blows to generate waves. At a constant wind speed, the longer the fetch, the larger the generated waves, up to an equilibrium point beyond which there is no further wave growth unless the wind speed increases. Figure 17 shows a proposed site for a shore protection project. The critical fetch must be determined in order to estimate the design wave height. The longest fetch is labeled (1) the figure. Line (2), although shorter than Line (2) crosses significantly deeper water.

In general, greater depths along the fetch will cause greater wave heights because of decreased bottom frictional effects. The fetch lines on Figure 17 have been divided into a series of equal length segments. As shown on the figure, by noting the depth at each division point, the average depth along the fetch can be determined. Care should be taken, however, to avoid including depths which are the result of small-scale depressions or rises, that are not typical of the area, but which the fetch line happens to cross. Small features such as rocks would not significantly affect wave growth and should be excluded in favor of a depth that is more typical to that area. The average depth must also be adjusted to correspond with the design water level. If, for instance, the design water level is +2.8 feet MLW, then the average fetch depth would be 10.0 feet for Line (1) and 14.4 feet for Line (2).

The final step in determining wind-driven wave heights is to refer to Tables 5, 6, 7, 8, and 9, and select the tables that bracket the average fetch depth. The wave height can then be found by using the fetch length and the fastest-mile wind speed. In the example, fetch line was 3.2 miles long with an average depth of 10.0 feet (design water level at +2.81 MLW). Assuming a 10-year, fastest-mile wind speed of 65 mi s/hour, the wave height would be 3.0 feet (Table 6). Along Line with an average depth of 14.4 feet, the wave height would b .5 feet (interpolating between Tables 6 and 7), despite the fact that its fetch length is only 2.4 miles. This should be used for design. The wave periods are given in parentheses on the tables below the wave heights. In both cases, the wave period is 4.0 seconds.

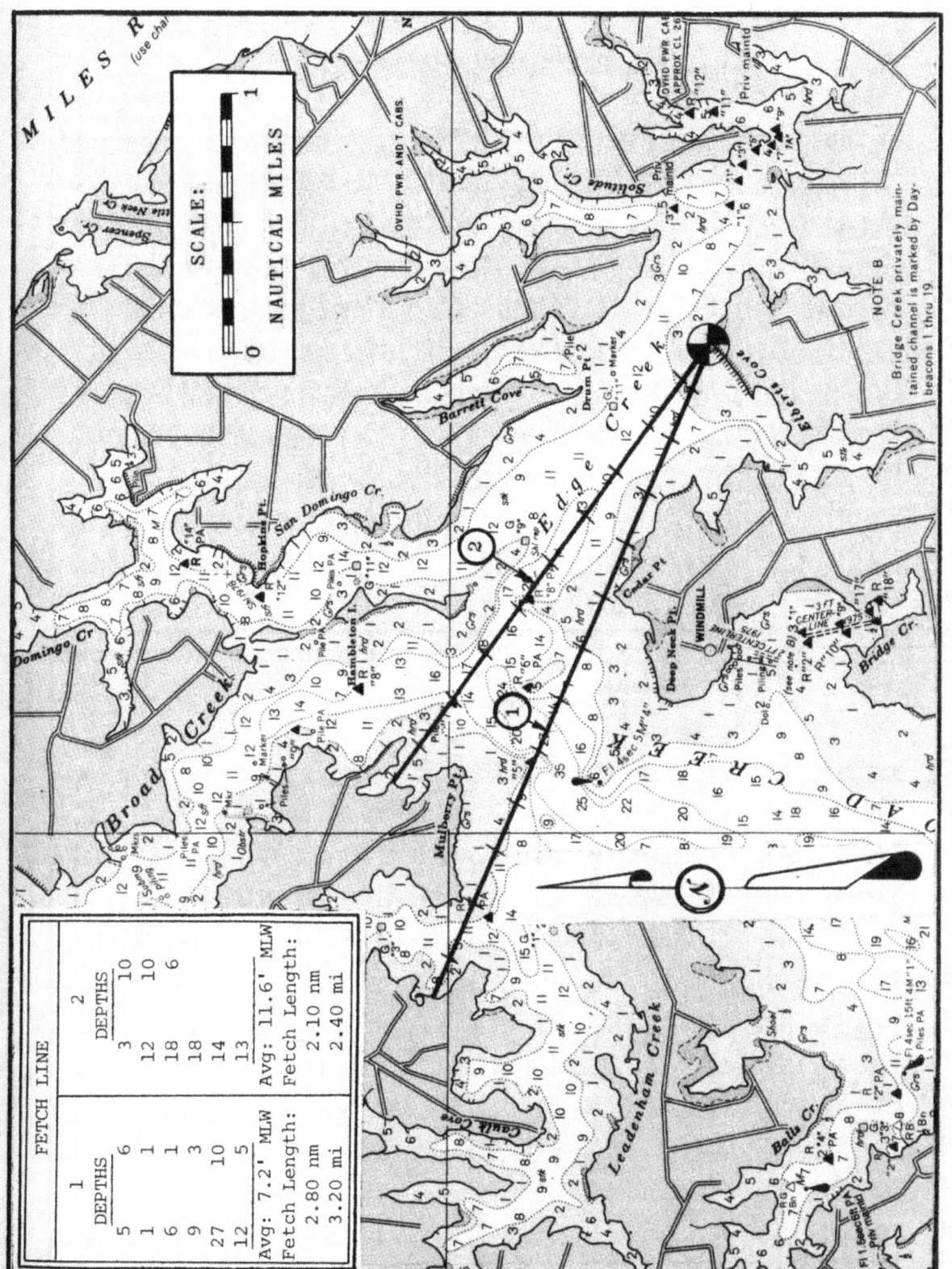

Figure 17   Identification of Fetch Lengths at a Site

Table 5

WIND-GENERATED WAVE HEIGHTS AND (PERIODS)
FETCH LENGTHS WITH AVERAGE DEPTHS = 5 FEET

Wind Speed (mph)	0.5	1.0	1.5	2.0	2.5	3.0	3.5	4.0	4.5	5.0	6.0	7.0	8.0	9.0	10.0
10	0.5 (1.0)	0.5 (1.0)	0.5 (1.0)	0.5 (2.0)	0.5 (2.0)	0.5 (2.0)	0.5 (2.0)	0.5 (2.0)	0.5 (2.0)	0.5 (2.0)	0.5 (2.0)	0.5 (2.0)	0.5 (2.0)	0.5 (2.0)	0.5 (2.0)
20	0.5 (1.0)	0.5 (2.0)	1.0 (2.0)	1.0 (2.0)	1.0 (2.0)	1.0 (2.0)	1.0 (2.0)	1.0 (2.0)	1.0 (2.0)	1.0 (2.0)	1.0 (2.0)	1.0 (2.0)	1.0 (2.0)	1.0 (2.0)	1.0 (2.0)
30	1.0 (2.0)	1.0 (2.0)	1.0 (2.0)	1.0 (2.0)	1.5 (2.0)	1.5 (3.0)	1.5 (3.0)	1.5 (3.0)	1.5 (3.0)	1.5 (3.0)	1.5 (3.0)	1.5 (3.0)	1.5 (3.0)	1.5 (3.0)	1.5 (3.0)
40	1.0 (2.0)	1.5 (2.0)	1.5 (3.0)	1.5 (3.0)	1.5 (3.0)	1.5 (3.0)	1.5 (3.0)	1.5 (3.0)	1.5 (3.0)	1.5 (3.0)	1.5 (3.0)	1.5 (3.0)	1.5 (3.0)	1.5 (3.0)	1.5 (3.0)
50	1.5 (2.0)	1.5 (3.0)	1.5 (3.0)	1.5 (3.0)	1.5 (3.0)	2.0 (3.0)	2.0 (3.0)	2.0 (3.0)	2.0 (3.0)	2.0 (3.0)	2.0 (3.0)	2.0 (3.0)	2.0 (3.0)	2.0 (3.0)	2.0 (3.0)
55	1.5 (2.0)	1.5 (3.0)	2.0 (3.0)	2.0 (3.0)	2.0 (3.0)	2.0 (3.0)	2.0 (3.0)	2.0 (3.0)	2.0 (3.0)	2.0 (3.0)	2.0 (3.0)	2.0 (3.0)	2.0 (3.0)	2.0 (3.0)	2.0 (3.0)
60	1.5 (2.0)	2.0 (3.0)	2.0 (3.0)	2.0 (3.0)	2.0 (3.0)	2.0 (3.0)	2.0 (3.0)	2.0 (3.0)	2.0 (3.0)	2.0 (3.0)	2.0 (3.0)	2.0 (4.0)	2.0 (4.0)	2.0 (4.0)	2.0 (4.0)
65	1.5 (3.0)	2.0 (3.0)	2.0 (3.0)	2.0 (3.0)	2.0 (3.0)	2.0 (3.0)	2.0 (3.0)	2.0 (3.0)	2.0 (3.0)	2.0 (4.0)	2.0 (4.0)	2.0 (4.0)	2.0 (4.0)	2.0 (4.0)	2.0 (4.0)
70	2.0 (3.0)	2.0 (3.0)	2.0 (3.0)	2.0 (3.0)	2.0 (3.0)	2.0 (3.0)	2.0 (3.0)	2.0 (4.0)	2.0 (4.0)	2.0 (4.0)	2.0 (4.0)	2.0 (4.0)	2.0 (4.0)	2.0 (4.0)	2.0 (4.0)
75	2.0 (3.0)	2.0 (3.0)	2.0 (3.0)	2.0 (3.0)	2.0 (3.0)	2.0 (3.0)	2.0 (4.0)	2.0 (4.0)	2.0 (4.0)	2.0 (4.0)	2.0 (4.0)	2.0 (4.0)	2.0 (4.0)	2.0 (4.0)	2.0 (4.0)
80	2.0 (3.0)	2.0 (3.0)	2.0 (3.0)	2.5 (3.0)	2.5 (3.0)	2.5 (4.0)	2.5 (4.0)	2.5 (4.0)	2.5 (4.0)	2.5 (4.0)	2.5 (4.0)	2.5 (4.0)	2.5 (4.0)	2.5 (4.0)	2.5 (4.0)

Table 6

WIND-GENERATED WAVE HEIGHTS AND (PERIODS)
FETCH LENGTHS WITH AVERAGE DEPTHS = 10 FEET

Wind Speed (mph)	0.5	1.0	1.5	2.0	2.5	3.0	3.5	4.0	4.5	5.0	6.0	7.0	8.0	9.0	10.0
10	0.5 (1.0)	0.5 (1.0)	0.5 (1.0)	0.5 (2.0)	0.5 (2.0)	0.5 (2.0)	0.5 (2.0)	0.5 (2.0)	0.5 (2.0)	0.5 (2.0)	0.5 (2.0)	0.5 (2.0)	1.0 (2.0)	1.0 (2.0)	1.0 (2.0)
20	0.5 (2.0)	1.0 (2.0)	1.0 (2.0)	1.0 (2.0)	1.0 (2.0)	1.0 (2.0)	1.0 (2.0)	1.5 (2.0)	1.5 (2.0)	1.5 (2.0)	1.5 (2.0)	1.5 (3.0)	1.5 (3.0)	1.5 (3.0)	1.5 (3.0)
30	1.0 (2.0)	1.5 (2.0)	1.5 (2.0)	1.5 (3.0)	1.5 (3.0)	1.5 (3.0)	2.0 (3.0)	2.0 (3.0)	2.0 (3.0)	2.0 (3.0)	2.0 (3.0)	2.0 (3.0)	2.0 (3.0)	2.0 (3.0)	2.0 (3.0)
40	1.5 (2.0)	1.5 (2.0)	2.0 (3.0)	2.0 (3.0)	2.0 (3.0)	2.0 (3.0)	2.5 (3.0)	2.5 (3.0)	2.5 (3.0)	2.5 (3.0)	2.5 (3.0)	2.5 (3.0)	2.5 (4.0)	2.5 (4.0)	2.5 (4.0)
50	1.5 (2.0)	2.0 (3.0)	2.5 (3.0)	2.5 (3.0)	2.5 (3.0)	2.5 (3.0)	2.5 (3.0)	2.5 (4.0)	3.0 (4.0)	3.0 (4.0)	3.0 (4.0)	3.0 (4.0)	3.0 (4.0)	3.0 (4.0)	3.0 (4.0)
55	2.0 (3.0)	2.5 (3.0)	2.5 (3.0)	2.5 (3.0)	2.5 (3.0)	3.0 (4.0)	3.0 (4.0)	3.0 (4.0)	3.0 (4.0)	3.0 (4.0)	3.0 (4.0)	3.0 (4.0)	3.0 (4.0)	3.0 (4.0)	3.0 (4.0)
60	2.0 (3.0)	2.5 (3.0)	2.5 (3.0)	3.0 (4.0)	3.0 (4.0)	3.0 (4.0)	3.0 (4.0)	3.0 (4.0)	3.0 (4.0)	3.0 (4.0)	3.0 (4.0)	3.0 (4.0)	3.5 (4.0)	3.5 (4.0)	3.5 (4.0)
65	2.0 (3.0)	2.5 (3.0)	3.0 (3.0)	3.0 (4.0)	3.0 (4.0)	3.0 (4.0)	3.0 (4.0)	3.5 (4.0)	3.5 (4.0)	3.5 (4.0)	3.5 (4.0)	3.5 (4.0)	3.5 (4.0)	3.5 (4.0)	3.5 (4.0)
70	2.5 (3.0)	3.0 (3.0)	3.0 (3.0)	3.0 (4.0)	3.5 (4.0)	3.5 (4.0)	3.5 (4.0)	3.5 (4.0)	3.5 (4.0)	3.5 (4.0)	3.5 (4.0)	3.5 (4.0)	3.5 (4.0)	3.5 (4.0)	3.5 (4.0)
75	2.5 (3.0)	3.0 (3.0)	3.0 (3.0)	3.5 (4.0)	3.5 (4.0)	3.5 (4.0)	3.5 (4.0)	3.5 (4.0)	3.5 (4.0)	3.5 (4.0)	3.5 (4.0)	3.5 (4.0)	3.5 (4.0)	3.5 (4.0)	3.5 (4.0)
80	2.5 (3.0)	3.0 (3.0)	3.5 (4.0)	3.5 (4.0)	3.5 (4.0)	3.5 (4.0)	3.5 (4.0)	3.5 (4.0)	3.5 (5.0)	4.0 (5.0)	4.0 (5.0)	4.0 (5.0)	4.0 (5.0)	4.0 (5.0)	4.0 (5.0)

Table 7

WIND-GENERATED WAVE HEIGHTS AND (PERIODS)
FETCH LENGTHS WITH AVERAGE DEPTHS = 15 FEET

Wind Speed (mph)	0.5	1.0	1.5	2.0	2.5	3.0	3.5	4.0	4.5	5.0	6.0	7.0	8.0	9.0	10.0
10	0.5 (1.0)	0.5 (1.0)	0.5 (1.0)	0.5 (2.0)	0.5 (2.0)	0.5 (2.0)	0.5 (2.0)	0.5 (2.0)	0.5 (2.0)	0.5 (2.0)	0.5 (2.0)	1.0 (2.0)	1.0 (2.0)	1.0 (2.0)	1.0 (2.0)
20	0.5 (2.0)	1.0 (2.0)	1.0 (2.0)	1.0 (2.0)	1.0 (2.0)	1.5 (2.0)	1.5 (2.0)	1.5 (2.0)	1.5 (2.0)	1.5 (2.0)	1.5 (2.0)	1.5 (3.0)	1.5 (3.0)	2.0 (3.0)	2.0 (3.0)
30	1.0 (2.0)	1.5 (2.0)	1.5 (2.0)	1.5 (3.0)	2.0 (3.0)	2.0 (3.0)	2.0 (3.0)	2.0 (3.0)	2.0 (3.0)	2.0 (3.0)	2.5 (3.0)	2.5 (3.0)	2.5 (3.0)	2.5 (3.0)	2.5 (3.0)
40	1.5 (2.0)	2.0 (3.0)	2.0 (3.0)	2.0 (3.0)	2.5 (3.0)	2.5 (3.0)	2.5 (3.0)	2.5 (3.0)	3.0 (3.0)	3.0 (3.0)	3.0 (4.0)	3.0 (4.0)	3.0 (4.0)	3.0 (4.0)	3.0 (4.0)
50	2.0 (2.0)	2.0 (3.0)	2.5 (3.0)	2.5 (4.0)	3.0 (4.0)	3.0 (4.0)	3.0 (4.0)	3.5 (4.0)	3.5 (4.0)	3.5 (4.0)	3.5 (4.0)	3.5 (4.0)	3.5 (4.0)	3.5 (4.0)	4.0 (4.0)
55	2.0 (3.0)	2.5 (3.0)	3.0 (3.0)	3.0 (4.0)	3.0 (4.0)	3.5 (4.0)	3.5 (4.0)	3.5 (4.0)	3.5 (4.0)	3.5 (4.0)	4.0 (4.0)	4.0 (4.0)	4.0 (4.0)	4.0 (4.0)	4.0 (4.0)
60	2.0 (3.0)	2.5 (3.0)	3.0 (3.0)	3.5 (4.0)	3.5 (4.0)	3.5 (4.0)	3.5 (4.0)	4.0 (4.0)	4.0 (4.0)	4.0 (4.0)	4.0 (4.0)	4.0 (4.0)	4.0 (4.0)	4.0 (5.0)	4.5 (5.0)
65	2.5 (3.0)	3.0 (3.0)	3.5 (3.0)	3.5 (4.0)	3.5 (4.0)	4.0 (4.0)	4.0 (4.0)	4.0 (4.0)	4.0 (4.0)	4.0 (4.0)	4.5 (4.0)	4.5 (4.0)	4.5 (4.0)	4.5 (5.0)	4.5 (5.0)
70	2.5 (3.0)	3.0 (3.0)	3.5 (4.0)	4.0 (4.0)	4.0 (4.0)	4.0 (4.0)	4.0 (4.0)	4.5 (4.0)	4.5 (4.0)	4.5 (4.0)	4.5 (5.0)	4.5 (5.0)	4.5 (5.0)	4.5 (5.0)	4.5 (5.0)
75	2.5 (3.0)	3.5 (3.0)	3.5 (4.0)	4.0 (4.0)	4.0 (4.0)	4.5 (4.0)	4.5 (4.0)	4.5 (4.0)	4.5 (4.0)	4.5 (4.0)	4.5 (5.0)	5.0 (5.0)	5.0 (5.0)	5.0 (5.0)	5.0 (5.0)
80	3.0 (3.0)	3.5 (4.0)	4.0 (4.0)	4.0 (4.0)	4.5 (4.0)	4.5 (4.0)	4.5 (4.0)	4.5 (5.0)	5.0 (5.0)	5.0 (5.0)	5.0 (5.0)	5.0 (5.0)	5.0 (5.0)	5.0 (5.0)	5.0 (5.0)

Table 8

WIND-GENERATED WAVE HEIGHTS AND (PERIODS)
FETCH LENGTHS WITH AVERAGE DEPTHS = 20 FEET

Wind Speed (mph)	0.5	1.0	1.5	2.0	2.5	3.0	3.5	4.0	4.5	5.0	6.0	7.0	8.0	9.0	10.0
10	0.5 (1.0)	0.5 (1.0)	0.5 (1.0)	0.5 (2.0)	0.5 (2.0)	0.5 (2.0)	0.5 (2.0)	0.5 (2.0)	0.5 (2.0)	0.5 (2.0)	1.0 (2.0)	1.0 (2.0)	1.0 (2.0)	1.0 (2.0)	1.0 (2.0)
20	0.5 (2.0)	1.0 (2.0)	1.0 (2.0)	1.0 (2.0)	1.0 (2.0)	1.5 (2.0)	1.5 (2.0)	1.5 (3.0)	1.5 (3.0)	1.5 (3.0)	1.5 (3.0)	1.5 (3.0)	2.0 (3.0)	2.0 (3.0)	2.0 (3.0)
30	1.0 (2.0)	1.5 (2.0)	1.5 (3.0)	1.5 (3.0)	2.0 (3.0)	2.0 (3.0)	2.0 (3.0)	2.0 (3.0)	2.5 (3.0)	2.5 (3.0)	2.5 (3.0)	2.5 (3.0)	3.0 (3.0)	3.0 (4.0)	3.0 (4.0)
40	1.5 (2.0)	2.0 (3.0)	2.0 (3.0)	2.5 (3.0)	2.5 (3.0)	2.5 (3.0)	3.0 (3.0)	3.0 (4.0)	3.0 (4.0)	3.0 (4.0)	3.5 (4.0)	3.5 (4.0)	3.5 (4.0)	3.5 (4.0)	3.5 (4.0)
50	2.0 (3.0)	2.5 (3.0)	2.5 (3.0)	3.0 (4.0)	3.0 (4.0)	3.5 (4.0)	3.5 (4.0)	3.5 (4.0)	3.5 (4.0)	4.0 (4.0)	4.0 (4.0)	4.0 (4.0)	4.0 (4.0)	4.5 (4.0)	4.5 (4.0)
55	2.0 (3.0)	2.5 (3.0)	3.0 (3.0)	3.0 (4.0)	3.5 (4.0)	3.5 (4.0)	4.0 (4.0)	4.0 (4.0)	4.0 (4.0)	4.0 (4.0)	4.5 (4.0)	4.5 (4.0)	4.5 (5.0)	4.5 (5.0)	4.5 (5.0)
60	2.0 (3.0)	3.0 (3.0)	3.0 (4.0)	3.5 (4.0)	4.0 (4.0)	4.0 (4.0)	4.0 (4.0)	4.0 (4.0)	4.5 (4.0)	4.5 (4.0)	4.5 (5.0)	5.0 (5.0)	5.0 (5.0)	5.0 (5.0)	5.0 (5.0)
65	2.5 (3.0)	3.0 (3.0)	3.5 (4.0)	4.0 (4.0)	4.0 (4.0)	4.5 (4.0)	4.5 (4.0)	4.5 (4.0)	4.5 (4.0)	5.0 (5.0)	5.0 (5.0)	5.0 (5.0)	5.0 (5.0)	5.0 (5.0)	5.5 (5.0)
70	2.5 (3.0)	3.5 (4.0)	4.0 (4.0)	4.0 (4.0)	4.5 (4.0)	4.5 (4.0)	4.5 (4.0)	5.0 (5.0)	5.0 (5.0)	5.0 (5.0)	5.0 (5.0)	5.5 (5.0)	5.5 (5.0)	5.5 (5.0)	5.5 (5.0)
75	3.0 (3.0)	3.5 (4.0)	4.0 (4.0)	4.5 (4.0)	4.5 (4.0)	5.0 (4.0)	5.0 (5.0)	5.0 (5.0)	5.0 (5.0)	5.5 (5.0)	5.5 (5.0)	5.5 (5.0)	5.5 (5.0)	6.0 (5.0)	6.0 (5.0)
80	3.0 (3.0)	4.0 (4.0)	4.5 (4.0)	4.5 (4.0)	5.0 (4.0)	5.0 (5.0)	5.5 (5.0)	5.5 (5.0)	5.5 (5.0)	5.5 (5.0)	5.5 (5.0)	6.0 (5.0)	6.0 (5.0)	6.0 (5.0)	6.0 (5.0)

Table 9

WIND-GENERATED WAVE HEIGHTS AND (PERIODS)
FETCH LENGTHS WITH AVERAGE DEPTHS = 25 FEET

Wind Speed (mph)	Fetch Length (miles)														
	0.5	1.0	1.5	2.0	2.5	3.0	3.5	4.0	4.5	5.0	6.0	7.0	8.0	9.0	10.0
10	0.5	0.5	0.5	0.5	0.5	0.5	0.5	0.5	0.5	0.5	1.0	1.0	1.0	1.0	1.0
	(1.0)	(1.0)	(1.0)	(2.0)	(2.0)	(2.0)	(2.0)	(2.0)	(2.0)	(2.0)	(2.0)	(2.0)	(2.0)	(2.0)	(2.0)
20	0.5	1.0	1.0	1.0	1.0	1.5	1.5	1.5	1.5	1.5	1.5	2.0	2.0	2.0	2.0
	(2.0)	(2.0)	(2.0)	(2.0)	(2.0)	(2.0)	(2.0)	(3.0)	(3.0)	(3.0)	(3.0)	(3.0)	(3.0)	(3.0)	(3.0)
30	1.0	1.5	1.5	2.0	2.0	2.0	2.0	2.5	2.5	2.5	2.5	2.5	3.0	3.0	3.0
	(2.0)	(2.0)	(2.0)	(3.0)	(3.0)	(3.0)	(3.0)	(3.0)	(3.0)	(3.0)	(3.0)	(3.0)	(4.0)	(4.0)	(4.0)
40	1.5	2.0	2.0	2.5	2.5	3.0	3.0	3.0	3.0	3.5	3.5	3.5	4.0	4.0	4.0
	(2.0)	(3.0)	(3.0)	(3.0)	(3.0)	(3.0)	(3.0)	(4.0)	(4.0)	(4.0)	(4.0)	(4.0)	(4.0)	(4.0)	(4.0)
50	2.0	2.5	3.0	3.0	3.5	3.5	3.5	4.0	4.0	4.0	4.5	4.5	4.5	4.5	5.0
	(3.0)	(3.0)	(3.0)	(3.0)	(4.0)	(4.0)	(4.0)	(4.0)	(4.0)	(4.0)	(4.0)	(4.0)	(4.0)	(5.0)	(5.0)
55	2.0	2.5	3.0	3.5	3.5	4.0	4.0	4.0	4.5	4.5	4.5	5.0	5.0	5.0	5.0
	(3.0)	(3.0)	(3.0)	(4.0)	(4.0)	(4.0)	(4.0)	(4.0)	(4.0)	(4.0)	(4.0)	(5.0)	(5.0)	(5.0)	(5.0)
60	2.0	3.0	3.5	3.5	4.0	4.0	4.5	4.5	4.5	5.0	5.0	5.0	5.5	5.5	5.5
	(3.0)	(3.0)	(3.0)	(4.0)	(4.0)	(4.0)	(4.0)	(4.0)	(4.0)	(4.0)	(5.0)	(5.0)	(5.0)	(5.0)	(5.0)
65	2.5	3.0	3.5	4.0	4.5	4.5	4.5	5.0	5.0	5.0	5.5	5.5	5.5	6.0	6.0
	(3.0)	(3.0)	(4.0)	(4.0)	(4.0)	(4.0)	(4.0)	(5.0)	(5.0)	(5.0)	(5.0)	(5.0)	(5.0)	(5.0)	(5.0)
70	2.5	3.5	4.0	4.5	4.5	5.0	5.0	5.0	5.0	5.5	5.5	6.0	6.0	6.0	6.5
	(3.0)	(3.0)	(4.0)	(4.0)	(4.0)	(4.0)	(4.0)	(5.0)	(5.0)	(5.0)	(5.0)	(5.0)	(5.0)	(5.0)	(5.0)
75	3.0	3.5	4.0	4.5	4.5	5.0	5.5	5.5	5.5	6.0	6.0	6.0	6.5	6.5	6.5
	(3.0)	(3.0)	(4.0)	(4.0)	(4.0)	(4.0)	(5.0)	(5.0)	(5.0)	(5.0)	(5.0)	(5.0)	(5.0)	(5.0)	(5.0)
80	3.0	4.0	4.5	5.0	5.0	5.5	5.5	6.0	6.0	6.0	6.5	6.5	6.5	7.0	7.0
	(3.0)	(4.0)	(5.0)	(5.0)	(5.0)	(5.0)	(5.0)	(5.0)	(5.0)	(5.0)	(5.0)	(5.0)	(5.0)	(6.0)	(6.0)

Alternate, more precise, methods of determining the wave height and period by using shallow water wave forecasting equations are given in U. S. Army Corps of Engineers (1977c) (1981b) and (1981c). The two later references will eventually supersede the first and are preferred by many coastal engineering specialists. Their use, however, involves more elaborate procedures so, for the sake of brevity and simplicity, only the equations from the first reference will be given. Either the tables or the equations are adequate for design of low cost shore protection.

The wave height, H. is,

$$H = (0.283U^2/g) \tanh [0.530 (gd/U^2)^{0.75}] \tanh \{(0.0125(gF/U^2)^{0.42})/(\tanh[0.530(gd/U^2)^{0.75}])\} \qquad (5)$$

And the period, T, is

$$T = 2.40 (\pi U/g) \tanh [0.833(gd/U^2)^{0.375}] \tanh \{(0.077(gF/U^2)^{0.25})/(\tanh[0.833(gd/U^2)^{0.375}])\} \qquad (6)$$

Where U = the wind speed in feet/second;
$\quad$ F = the fetch length in feet;
$\quad$ D = the depth in feet:
And $\quad$ g= 32.2 ft/sec^2.

Note: The above equations are in dimensionless form and can be used with any consistent set of units.

Wave heights so determined should then be checked against the maximum possible breaking wave at the design water level. This should be evaluated using Figure 18 and the depth at the toe of the structure, or if appropriate, the minimum depth offshore from the structure. With the design water depth at the toe of the structure d_s; the wave period, T; and the fronting bottom slope, m; the breaker height H_b, can be found as a function of d_s. For instance, if d_s = 3.0 feet, m = 1:33, and T = 4.0 seconds d_s/gT^2 = 0.00582, and H_b/d_s = 0.98; therefore, H_b = 3.0 x 0.98 = 2 (say 3.0) feet. T. Minimum depth along fetch line is near Cedar Point where the depth is 1 foot at MLW, and 3.1 feet under the design water level. This would not control for this case (it is greater than d_s), but it should be checked in every instance. Fetch line (2) does not cross similar shoal areas.

If the wind-driven wave height was 3.5 feet, it should not be used for design because only a 3.0-foot wave can be supported based on the available minimum depth at the structure. The final design wave height, therefore, should be 2.9 (3.0) feet in this case. *To restate the rule, the design wave height should be the lesser of the maximum wind-generated wave along the fetch, or the maximum possible breaking wave at the structure or at points offshore.*

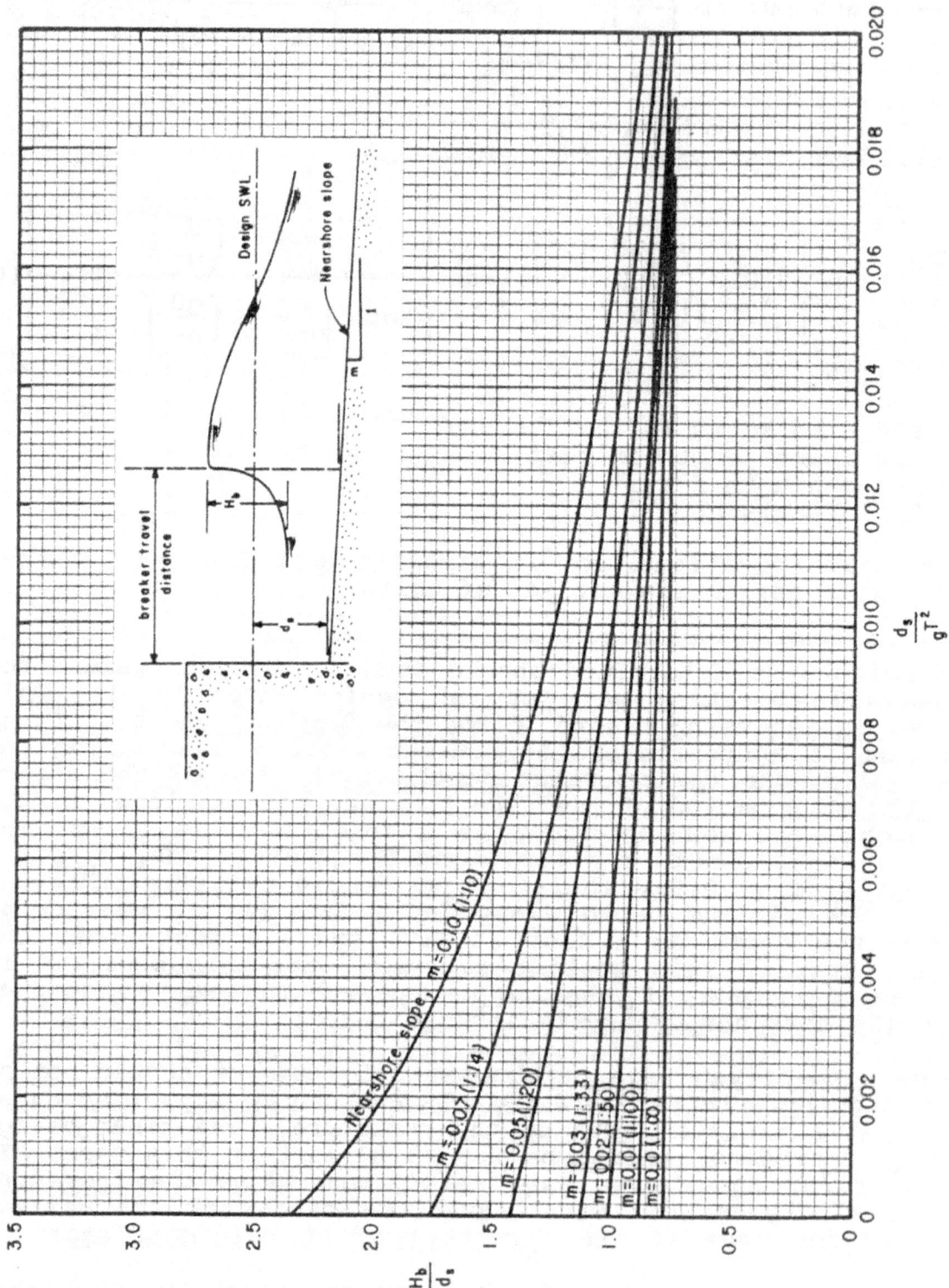

Figure 18   Dimensionless Design Breaker Height Versus Relative Depth at Structure
[Weggel (1972)]

Figure 19 gives appropriate locations for measuring the depth at the structure, d_s.

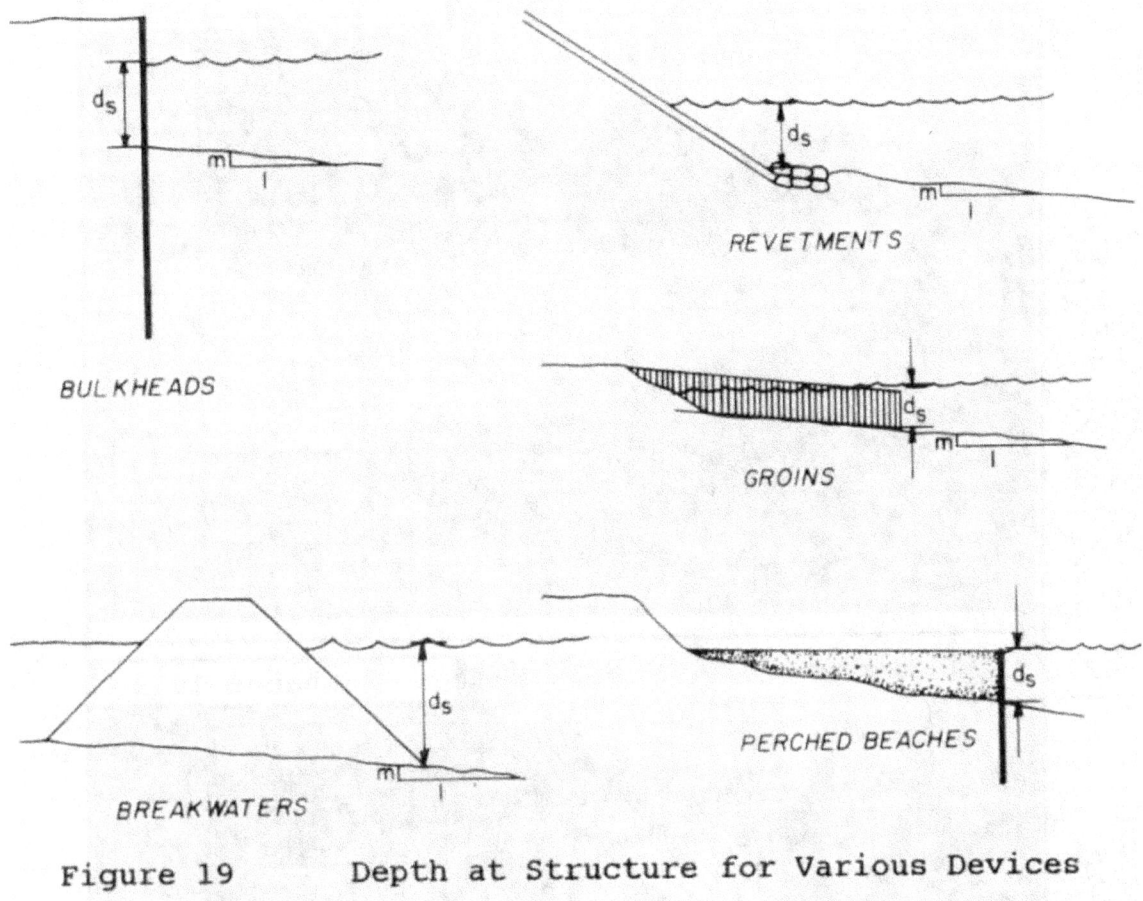

Figure 19   Depth at Structure for Various Devices

Strength

Shore protection structures must be strong, and this can only be achieved by using either massive and heavy components that cannot be dislodged by waves, or smaller components that interlock to form a large mass. The problem with small interlocking units, such as concrete blocks, is that they exhibit little reserve strength. That is, once damages occur, they generally progress to complete failure.

Flexibility

Flexibility is also desired because it allows structures to compensate for settlement, consolidation and toe scour. The revetment shown on Figure 20 illustrates this point. The massive individual concrete slabs could not be moved by waves, but the structure failed because it was not able to adjust to erosion that occurred around the ends and through cracks between the slabs.

Toe Protection

Toe protection is supplemental armoring of the beach surface in front of a structure, which prevents waves from scouring or undercutting it. Failure to provide toe protection invites almost certain failure.

Figure 20   Flexibility as a Structural Requirement

Filtering

Filtering, although one of the most important technical design details of shore protection structures, is probably the most neglected, and leads to more failures than any other cause. The consequences of not providing proper filtering are illustrated on Figure 22. Without filtering, the soil particles are easily transported through the armor layer, which continues to settle as the bank erodes. A properly designed filter blocks the passage of the soil particles while still allowing for hydrostatic pressure relief beneath the structure (Figure 23).

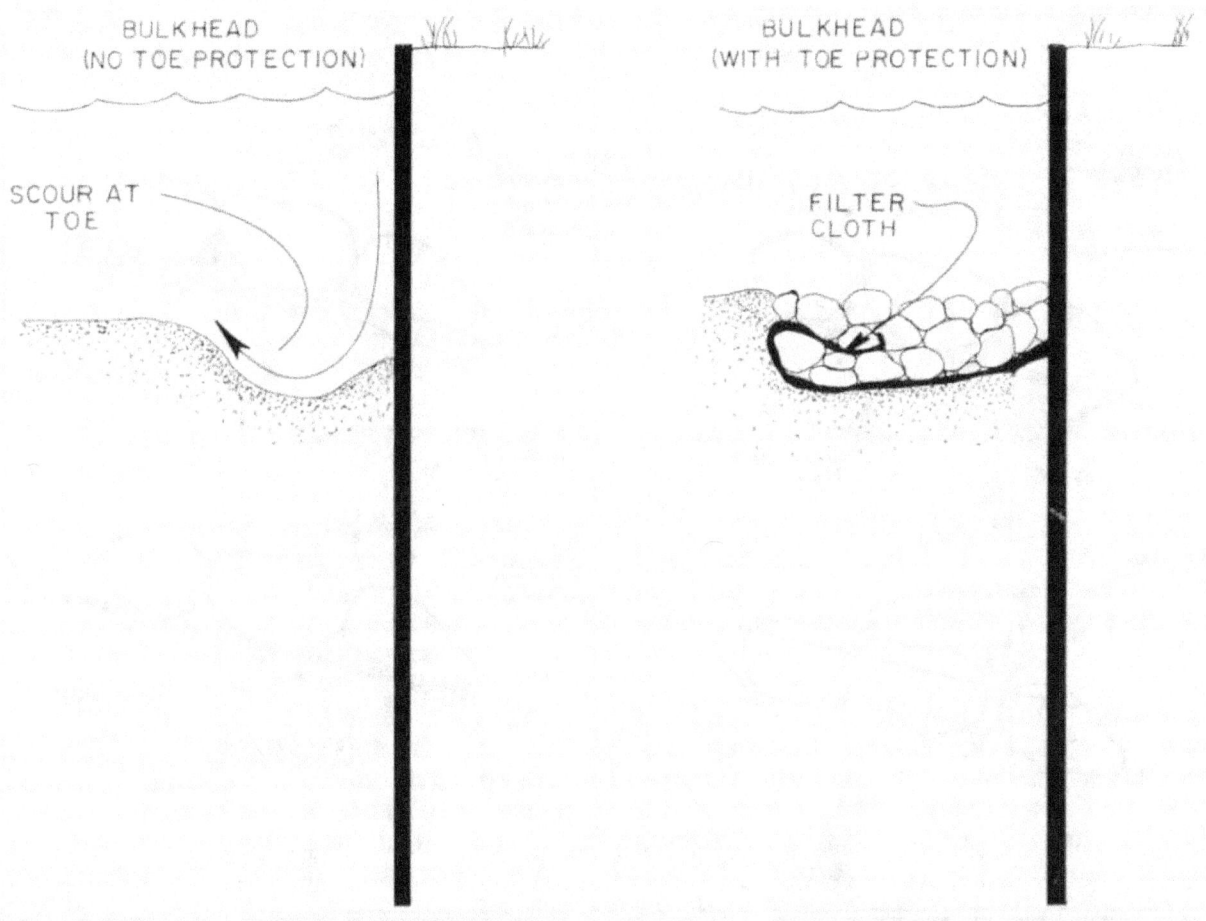

Figure 21   Typical Example of Toe Protection

A filter layer can be provided through the use of either graded aggregates or a synthetic filter fabric. Filter criteria for graded filters are covered in standard references such as Winterkorn and Fang (1975). Bertram (1940) developed one widely used criterion as given below:

$$D_{15} \text{(filter)}/D_{85} \text{(soil)} \quad < 4 \text{ to } 5 < D_{15} \text{(filter)}/ D_{15}\text{(soil)} \qquad (7)$$

The left side of the equation is intended to prevent piping of fine-grained soil through the filter. That is, the 15-percent size of the filter material, D_{15} (percent finer by weight), must be no more than 4 or 5 times the D_{85} size of the protected soil. The right side of the equation provides for adequate permeability of the filter (several times greater than the adjacent soil). It requires the D_{15} size of the filter to be at least 4 or 5 times the D_{15} of the soil. This criterion should provide adequate permeability for structural bedding layers, but be insufficient for the groundwater drains.

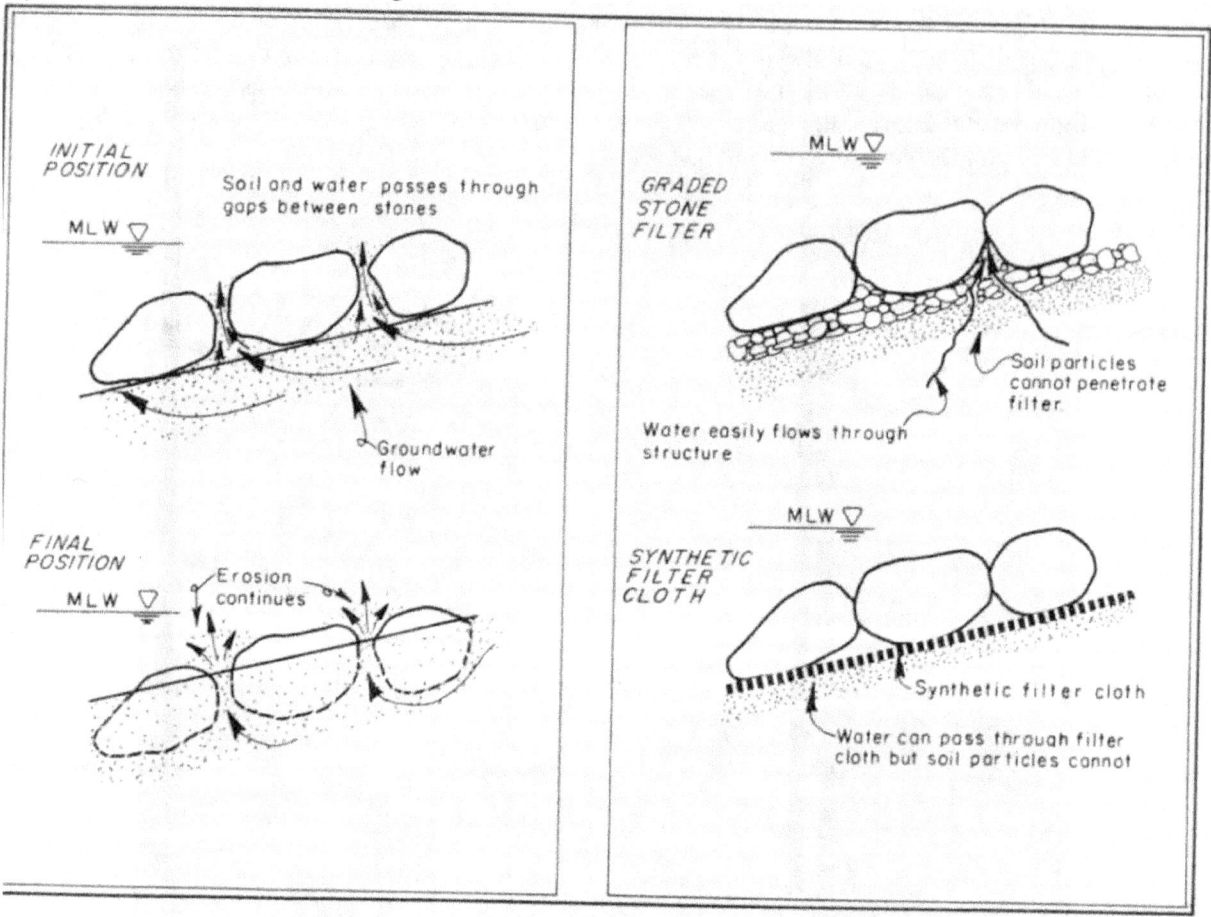

	Figure 22	Figure 23
	Inadequate or No Filtering	**Proper Filter Design**

Several organizations have developed further restrictive criteria for filters.   For instance, the Bureau of Reclamation allows no filter aggregates larger than 3.0 inches, and the Corps of Engineers specifies that,

$$D_{50}\,(\text{filter}) / D_{50}\,(\text{soil}) \;\; <= 25 \qquad (8)$$

In other words, the D_{50} of the filter cannot be greater than 25 times the D_{50} of the soil. This is intended to insure that the gradation curves of the filter and soil are generally parallel.

For perforated or slotted pipe, the D_{85} of the filter must be greater than the hole width or slot diameter.

$$D_{85} \text{ (filter) / Hole diameter} \quad > (1.0 \text{ to } 1.2) \qquad (9)$$

$$D_{85} \text{ (filter) / Slot width} \quad > (1.2 \text{ to } 1.4) \qquad (10)$$

These and other criteria for graded filters are illustrated on Figure 24.

The above criteria also apply to the armor layer in relation to the filter layer. That is, the armor layer must retain the filter layer as the filter retains the soil. In some cases, two filter layers may be required to provide the necessary transition from the soil to the armor.

Synthetic filter fabrics, available in woven and non-woven varieties, can be used in place of graded stone filters. Woven cloths, manufactured of high strength nylon or other synthetic fibers, provide a uniform mesh with a constant opening size which can be matched to the soil characteristics. Non-woven cloths, manufactured from masses of somewhat randomly oriented fibers bonded together by chemicals, heat or pressure,, come in various standard thicknesses. Unlike woven cloths, however, they lack uniform-sized openings, their principal advantage being lower cost.

Guidance on the selection of filter fabrics is contained in Plastic Filter Fabric [U. S. Army Corps of Engineers (1977a)]. Selection is based on the equivalent opening size (EOS), which the Corps defines as "the number of the U. S. Standard Sieve having openings closest in size to the filter fabric openings". Material will first be retained on the sieve whose number is equal to the EOS. The EOS of commonly used filter fabrics is given in Table 10. The appropriate filter fabric should be selected as follows:

For granular soils with less than 50 percent by weight fines
(minus **No.** 200 materials)

$$\frac{85\%, \text{ Passing Size of Soil}}{\text{Opening Size of the EOS Sieve}} \quad => 1 \qquad (11)$$

For other soils, the EOS should not be less than 70 (0.0083 in.). Furthermore, to reduce problems with clogging, no fabric should be used whose EOS is greater than 100 (openings smaller than the mesh of a No. 100 sieve). Also, no filter fabric should be used alone if the underlying soil contains more than 85 percent of particles finer than the No. 200 sieve. In those cases, an intermediate sand layer may provide the necessary transition layer from the in-situ soil to the filter fabric.

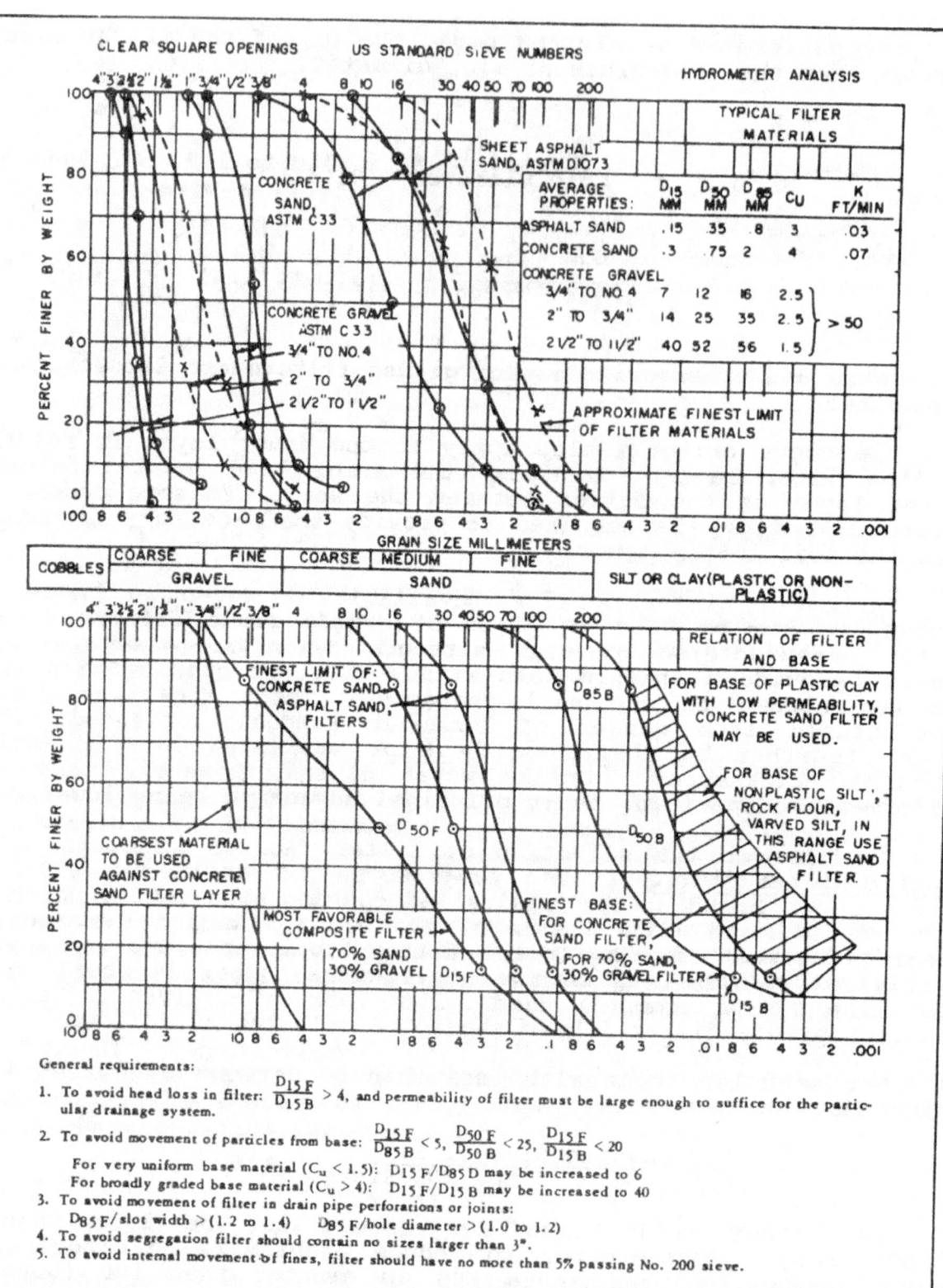

General requirements:

1. To avoid head loss in filter: $\frac{D_{15}F}{D_{15}B} > 4$, and permeability of filter must be large enough to suffice for the particular drainage system.

2. To avoid movement of particles from base: $\frac{D_{15}F}{D_{85}B} < 5$, $\frac{D_{50}F}{D_{50}B} < 25$, $\frac{D_{15}F}{D_{15}B} < 20$

   For very uniform base material ($C_u < 1.5$): $D_{15}F/D_{85}D$ may be increased to 6
   For broadly graded base material ($C_u > 4$): $D_{15}F/D_{15}B$ may be increased to 40

3. To avoid movement of filter in drain pipe perforations or joints:
   $D_{85}F/$slot width $> (1.2$ to $1.4)$ $D_{85}F/$hole diameter $> (1.0$ to $1.2)$

4. To avoid segregation filter should contain no sizes larger than 3".

5. To avoid internal movement of fines, filter should have no more than 5% passing No. 200 sieve.

Figure 24   Design Criteria for Protective Filters
[U.S. Navy, Naval Facilities Engineering Command (1971)]

Table 10	
FILTER FABRIC EQUIVALENT OPENING SIZES	
Fabric	EOS
Filter X	100
Laurel Erosion Control Cloth	100
Monsanto E2B	80
Polyfilter X	70
Mirafi 140	50
Nicolon 66424	50
Nicolon 66429	40
Polyfilter GB	40
Nicolon 66487	30

[U.S. Army Corps of Engineers (1977a)]

*Note: Manufacturer's product lines are subject to change. Check with the supplier to verify current products and specifications.

The Corps of Engineers also limits the gradient ratio of the filter fabric to a maximum of 3. This is defined as the hydraulic gradient through the fabric and the one inch of soil immediately above the fabric (i_1) divided by the hydraulic gradient over the two inches of soil 'between one and three inches above the fabric (i_2).

$$\text{Gradient Ratio} = i_1/i_2 \ <= 3, \qquad (12)$$

Where i_1 and i_2 are measured by a constant head permeability test conducted as specified by the Corps in the earlier cited reference.

Flank Protection

Flank protection is important because any shore protection structure, such as a revetment or bulkhead, is vulnerable as erosion continues around its ends. If not prevented by flank protection, the land eventually erodes from behind the structure, which then fails to function adequately. Figure 25 illustrates what happens when flank protection is not provided.

Return sections can be provided either during the original construction or later, as erosion progresses. For instance, sheet pile bulkheads along low bluffs can easily be tied into the existing bank during the initial work. This is not generally possible for high bluffs. Revetments must nearly always be progressively lengthened as erosion continues. They should be tied to the existing bank or high ground during initial construction, however.

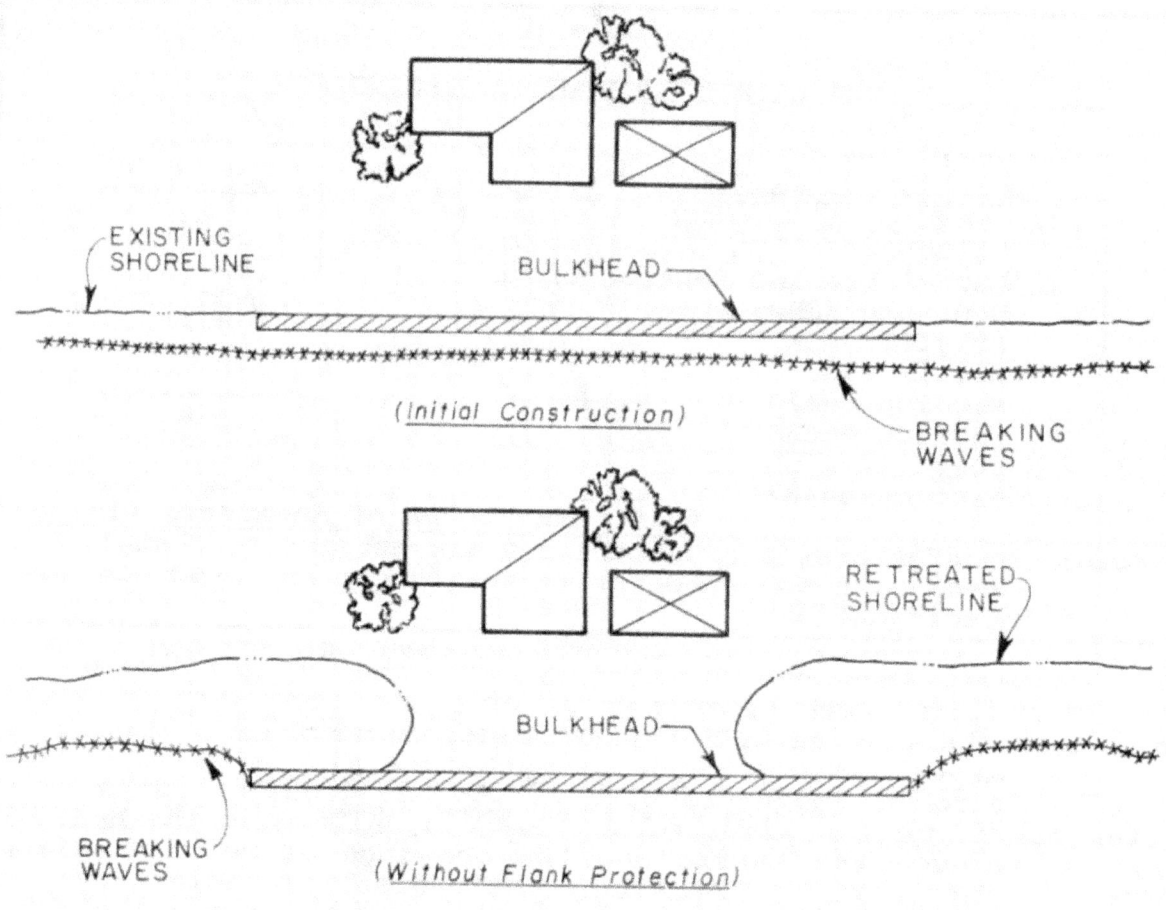

EXISTING
SHORELINE

BULKHEAD

(*Initial Construction*)

BREAKING
WAVES

RETREATED
SHORELINE

BULKHEAD

BREAKING
WAVES

(*Without Flank Protection*)

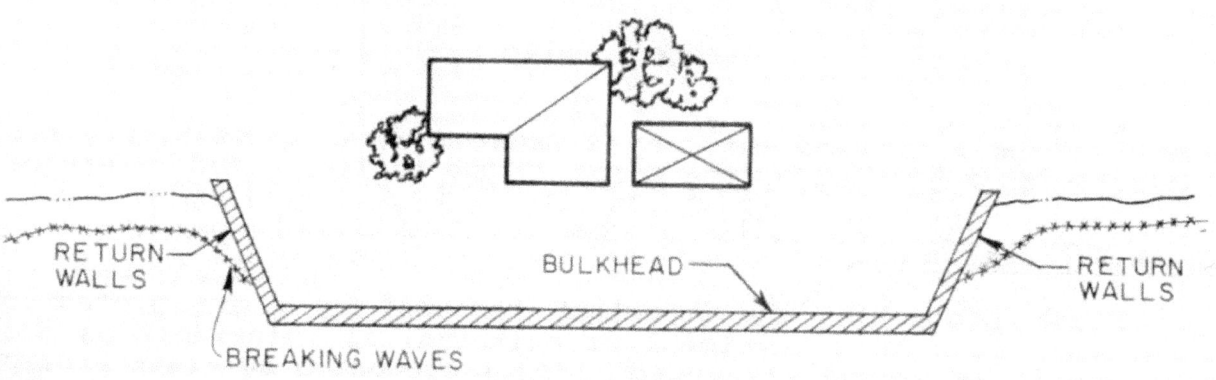

RETURN
WALLS

BULKHEAD

RETURN
WALLS

BREAKING WAVES

(*With Flank Protection*)

Figure 25   Flank Protection

Structure Height

Waves breaking against an inclined structure will run up to an elevation higher than the Stillwater level depending on the roughness of the structure. Smooth concrete surfaces experience higher runup than rough stone slopes. Vertical structures also cause splashing and can experience overtopping. If possible, the structure should be built high enough to preclude severe overtopping. White spray does little damage, but solid jets of "green" water should be avoided. The required height of the structure will depend on the computed runup height based on the wave and structure characteristics. Detailed guidance is presented in Stoa (1978) and (1979). The runup height, R, can be found by a more approximate method as given below.

First, find the wavelength at the structure by using either Figure 26 or Equation (3) with the known depth at the structure and the design wave period. The definition sketch for runup is shown on Figure 27. For SMOOTH impermeable slopes, the runup, R, is given in Seelig (1980) by,

$$R = HC_1 (0.12L/H)^{\wedge}(C_2 (H/d_s)^{0.5} + C_3)$$

where:
- L = the local wavelength from Figure 26 or Eq. (3),
- d_s = the depth at the structure (feet),
  the approaching wave height (feet), and
- C_1, C_2, C_3 = coefficients given below.

Structure Slope *	C_1	C_2	C_3
Vertical	0.96	0.23	+0.06
1 on 1.0	1.47	0.35	-0.11
1 on 1.5	1.99	0.50	-0.19
1 on 2.25	1.81	0.47	-0.08
1 on 3.0	1.37	0.51	+0.04

*Interpolate linearly between these values for other slopes.

For ROUGH slopes, Seelig (1980) gives the runup as,

$$R = (0.69\xi/1+0.5\xi)H \qquad (14)$$

$$\xi = \tan \theta/(H/L_o)^{0.5} \qquad (15)$$

$$L_o = 5.12 \, T^2 \qquad (16)$$

θ = structure of the slope (e. g., $\tan \theta = 0.25$ for a slope of 1V on 4H

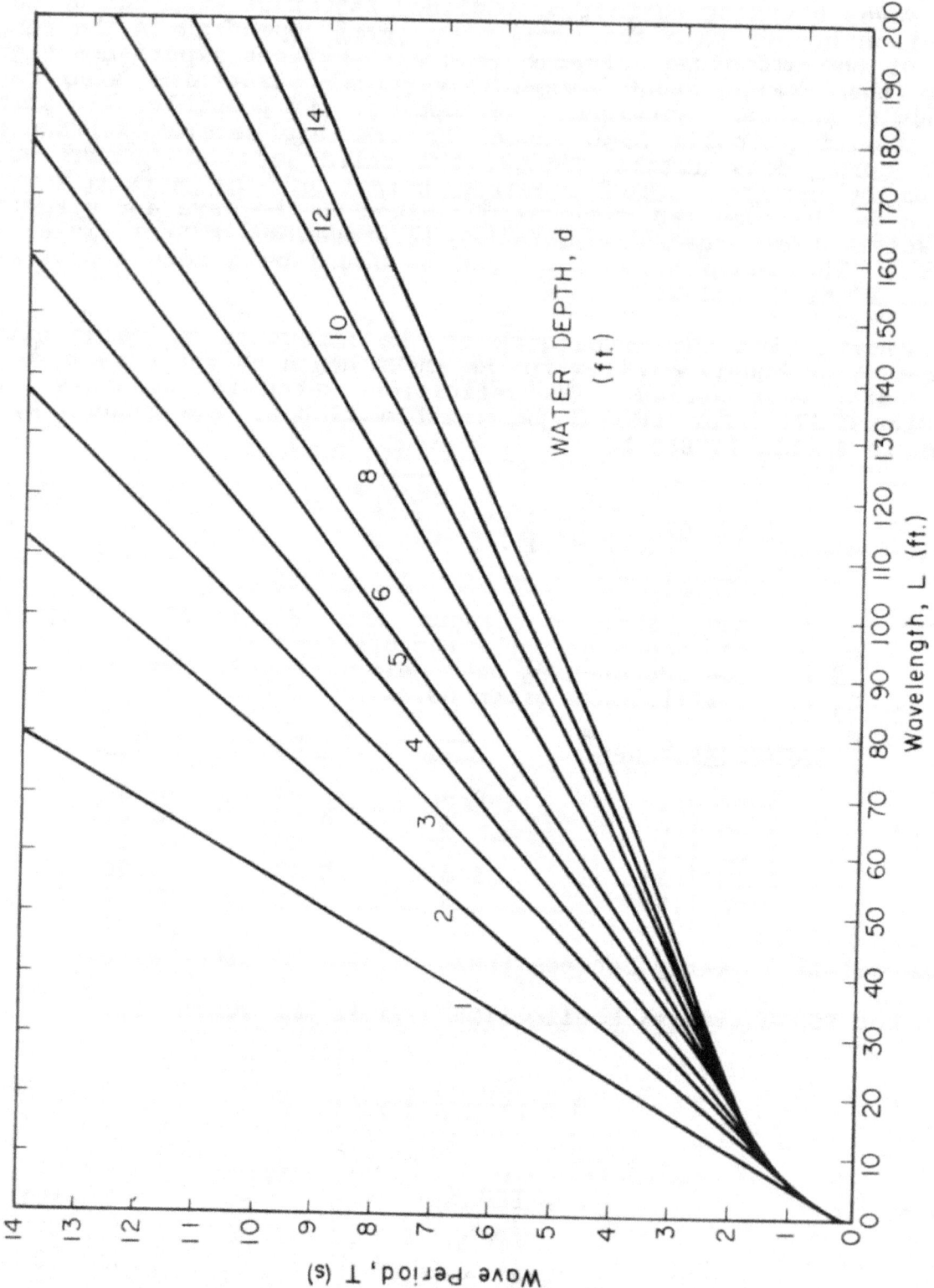

Figure 26   Local Wavelength Given Depth and Period
[After Giles and Eckert (1979)]

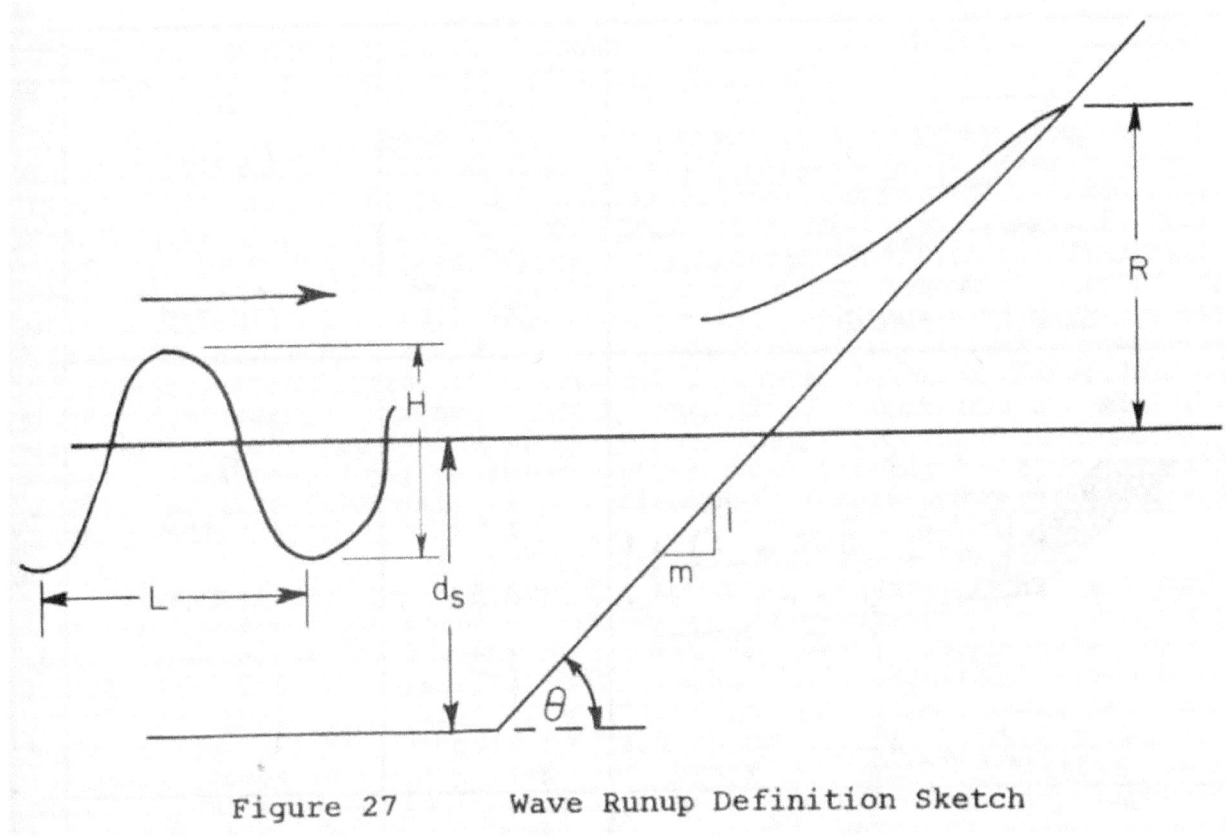

Figure 27   Wave Runup Definition Sketch

For STEPPED slopes, Stoa (1979) recommends using 70 to 75 percent of the smooth slope runup if the risers are vertical, and 86 percent if the edges are rounded.

A rough approximation of the runup height can be obtained from Table 11. However, the values in the table tend to represent the upper bound of the available data and may result in over design. Equations (13) and (14) or the methods given in Stoa (1978) and (1979) are recommended.

If it is impossible or undesirable to build a structure to the recommended height, a splash apron should be provided at the top of the structure. These are generally constructed of rock and they prevent the ground at the top from being eroded and undermining that portion of the structure.

Environmental Factors

Many different materials can be used to construct shore protection structures, including rock, concrete, timber, metal and plastics. The choice often depends on the desired permanence of the protection. Durable materials usually cost considerably more than shorter-lived materials used for temporary protection. The choice of materials is important because the coastal environment is a harsh testing ground for all man-made structures. Aside from wave forces, which are formidable in and of themselves, a host of chemical, biological and other factors can degrade structural materials. A brief review of these follows.

	m	R
SMOOTH FACE	1.5	2.25H
	2.5	1.75H
	4.0	1.50H

	m	R
ROUGH FACE	1.5	1.25H
	2.5	1.00H
	4.0	0.75H

	m	R
STEPPED FACE	1.5	2.00H

	m	R
VERTICAL FACE	—	2.00H

Table 11   Wave Runup Heights

Corrosion and Freezing. Corrosion is a primary problem with metals in brackish and saline water. This is particularly true in the splash zone, where the materials are subjected to continuous wet-dry cycles. Plain carbon steel, for instance, probably has a life of less than five years under some conditions. Corrosion resistant steel marketed under various trade names is useful for some applications. Aluminum sheet piling can also be used in many areas in place of steel. Stainless, galvanized, or other corrosion-protected steel, or wrought iron can be used for bolts and other fasteners. However, care should be taken not to mix dissimilar metals in structures where they directly contact each other. The resulting galvanic action will quickly corrode the more active metal of the pair (e.g., aluminum is more active than stainless steel).

Concrete can be degraded by chemical reaction with salt water and by freeze-thaw cycles. Guidance on producing suitable high quality concrete is presented in Mather (1957). Aggregates should be durable and not reactive with cement. Dense (cement rich) mixes should be used, typically about 7 bags of portland cement per cubic yard. Types II or V should be used in salt water, while Types I or II are acceptable in fresh and brackish water. Potable water should generally be used, but brackish or salt water may sometimes be acceptable for mass concrete. Fresh water, however, should always be used for reinforced concrete. Maximum water content should be no more than 5 1/2 gallons per bag of cement, including the moisture content of the aggregates. Finally, air entrainment (typically 4 to 7% of the concrete volume) is necessary to minimize damages from freeze-thaw cycles.

Marine Borer Activity. Timber structures submerged in brackish and sa-1 water are sub ' ject to damage from marine borers. Any wood or timber used for bulkhead or other construction in areas of moderate borer activity should be treated with 20 pounds of creosote or 2.5 lbs. of preservative salts per cubic foot of timber. Where borer activity is severe, 20 pounds of creosote and 1.5 pounds per cubic foot of preservative salts in a dual-treatment process is recommended for all lumber. Timber piles should be dual-treated with 20 pounds of creosote and 1.0 pound of preservative salts per cubic foot in such areas [American Wood Preservers' Association (1977)].

Ultraviolet Light. The ultraviolet component of sunlight rapidly degrades untreated synthetic fibers such as those used for filter cloth or sand bags, totally deteriorating them in less than one season if heavily exposed. Any fabric used for shore protection devices should be stabilized against ultraviolet light. This typically involves adding carbon black to the synthetic compound, which gives the finished product a black or dark color in contrast to the white or light gray color of unstabilized cloth. Even filter cloth covered by a structure should be stabilized since small cracks or openings in the structure could admit enough light to destroy the cloth.

Abrasion. Abrasion damage occurs in all structures where waves move coarse sediments such as sand and gravel back and forth across their faces. coarse gravels and cobbles can also cause impact damages when hurled by large waves. Little can be done to prevent abrasion damages beyond the use of durable rock and concrete as armoring in critical areas such as along the sand line of sheet pile groins. It is here that such structures typically experience the greatest amount of abrasion.

Ice Forces. Ice forces are primarily a problem on cold region waterbodies such as the Great Lakes. Ice covers will typically vary with the size and location of the waterbody, and local climatic conditions. Large bodies, such as the Great Lakes, usually develop partial ice covers, while smaller embayments within them may be totally covered.

The ice covets are never totally stationary and movement creates several categories of ice forces on structures. For instance, dynamic forces result from wind and current-driven ice sheets or floes.

Vertical-faced structures will experience large horizontal forces, while inclined faces will tend to reduce the total force acting on the structure. Static ice forces result from thermal 6xpansion and contraction of relatively stationary ice sheets. Fractured ice forces arise from broken pack ice driven against a structure. Uplift and drawdown forces are associated with the adhesion of floating ice sheets to structures.

Water level fluctuations caused by seiches, tides, or reservoir operation can result in significant damage to pile-supported structures. Water level recession can cause considerable downward loadings that force the piles deeper into the bottom. Conversely, water surface rises will pull the piles upward. As this occurs, the soil will collapse beneath the pile tips and will prevent return to their original positions. A series of such actions can jack the piles completely out of the bottom.

Possible preventative measures include air bubbler systems and pile sleeves, but these must be evaluated on an individual case basis. Relatively comprehensive summaries of current methods for evaluating ice forces on structures are given in Neill (1976), Wortley (1978) and the U. S. Army Corps of Engineers (1980b).

Vandalism and Theft. The final factor is the susceptibility of the structure to vandalism. If this may be a problem, materials should be selected which cannot easily be cut, carried away, dismantled or otherwise damaged. For instance, sand-filled fabric bags are easily slashed by knives, small concrete blocks can be stolen, and wire mesh baskets can be opened with wire cutters and the contents scattered.

SHORE PROTECTION METHODS

This section will examine specific devices, including structures and vegetation, in more detail. Where past performance data are available, these will be incorporated in the discussion.

BULKHEADS

Because bulkheads normally have vertical faces for ease of construction and cost efficiency, wave reflections are maximized, increasing the potential for overtopping and scour in front of the structure. Since scour can be a serious problem, toe protection is necessary for stability. Typical toe protection consists of quarrystone large enough to resist movement by wave forces, with an underlying layer of granular material or filter cloth to prevent the soil from being washed through voids in the scour apron.

Sheet Pile Bulkheads

Wave Height Range: Above five feet.

Sheet piling is available in different materials, including steel, aluminum and timber. These are used in structures that may be either cantilevers or anchored (Figure 28). Detailed design procedures are available in standard references such as the Steel Sheet Piling Design Manual [U. S. Steel Corporation (1975)].

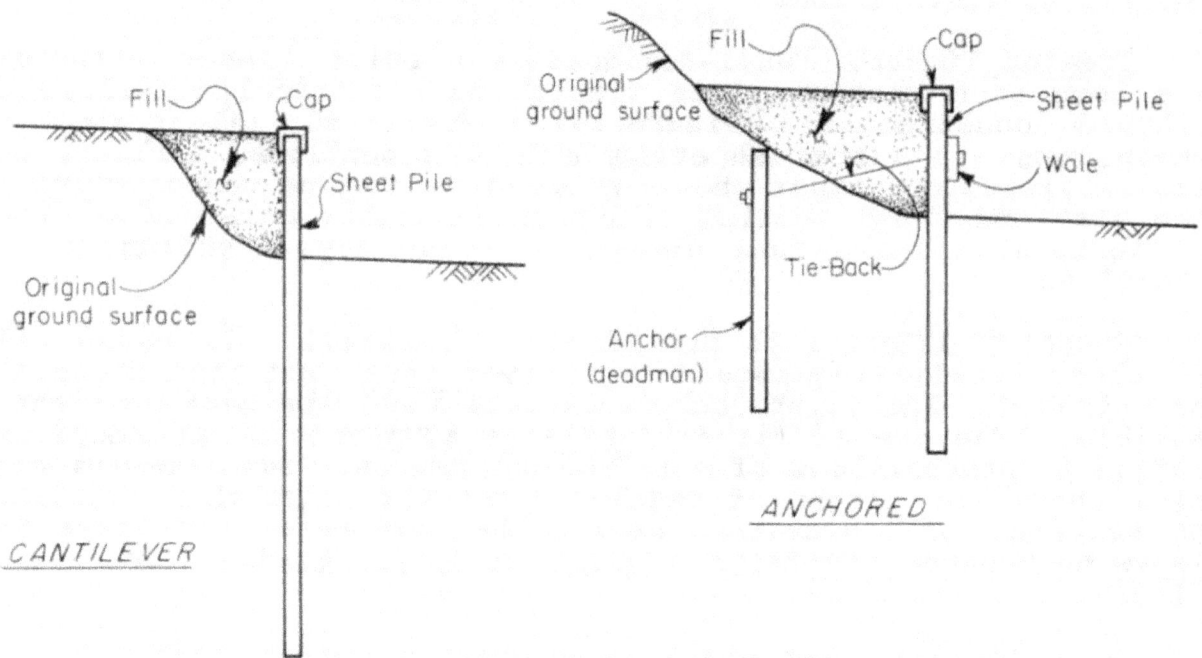

Figure 28   **Cantilever and Anchored Sheet Pile Bulkheads**

A cantilever bulkhead derives its support solely from ground penetration; therefore, the sheet piles must be driven deep enough to resist overturning. Cantilever bulkheads are susceptible failure due to toe scour because this reduces the effective embedment of the piling.

An anchored or braced bulkhead gains additional support against seaward def lection from embedded anchors or from batter structural piles on the seaward side. Anchors are commonly a r of piles or deadmen driven or buried a distance behind the bulkhead. Connections between the anchors and wall should be wrought iron, galvanized or other suitably corrosion-protected steel. Plain carbon steel should not be used for long-term protection. Horizontal wales are generally located in the upper one-third the wall height above the dredge line. For low bulkheads, they m be at or near the top of the structure. The wales distribute the anchors, the lateral loads on the structure. An anchor system is not well suited to sites with buildings close to the shoreline because of the distance needed between the bulkhead and anchor In that case, brace piles ma be used in lace of anchoring.

Subsurface conditions determine the type of sheet piling that can be used. Steel sheet piling can be driven into hard soil and some soft rock. Aluminum and timber sheet piling can only by driven or jetted into softer soil.

The advantages of sheet pile bulkheads are their relatively long and maintenance-free lives, and their uniform appearance. Their disadvantages include the special pile-driving equipment required to install them.

Treated Timber. Well-designed and built timber structures have long been recognized as viable and economical materials for bulkhead construction (Figure 29). Figure 30 illustrates the common types of timber sheeting used. As mentioned earlier, only specially treated timber should be used for marine construction. A plan view and cross section of a typical timber bulkhead are shown on Figure 31. The actual dimensions will vary depending on site conditions.

Granular material is preferred for backfill. If anchor piles are used, backfilling should begin over them, and then proceed to the bulkhead. The joints between sheets should be kept as tight as possible. The use of filter fabric is advisable as an added precaution to prevent loss of soil through cracks. Supplemental drain holes should be placed at regular intervals to further facilitate the movement of water from behind the structure, and these must always be backed with filter cloth or properly graded crushed-stone filters.

Figure 29   Timber Sheet Pile Bulkhead
(Photo Courtesy of Koppers Company, Inc.)

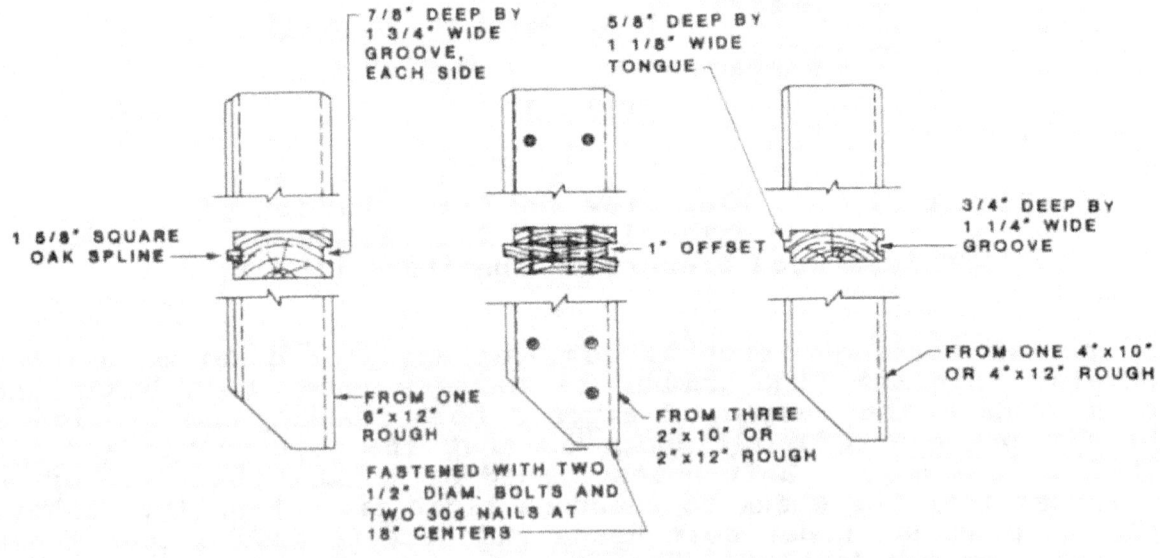

Figure 30   Typical Timber Sheet Sections
[Winterkorn and Fang (1975)]

Only corrosion-resistant or protected metals should be used for hardware and fasteners. Wrought iron anchor rods with turnbuckles and bolts have good durability. Galvanized fasteners are also recommended. Carbon steel should not be used unless protected with special coatings, such as coal-tar epoxy or other bituminous materials. Minimize the number of washers under bolt heads and nuts to reduce the length of exposed bolt shanks, and provide a tight fit between bolted timbers so that the bolt shanks are not exposed in the gaps. Bolt holes should be no more than 1/16 of an inch larger than the shank to insure a tight fit. Finally, washers should be provided under bolt heads and nuts to insure that these bear evenly on the timber members.

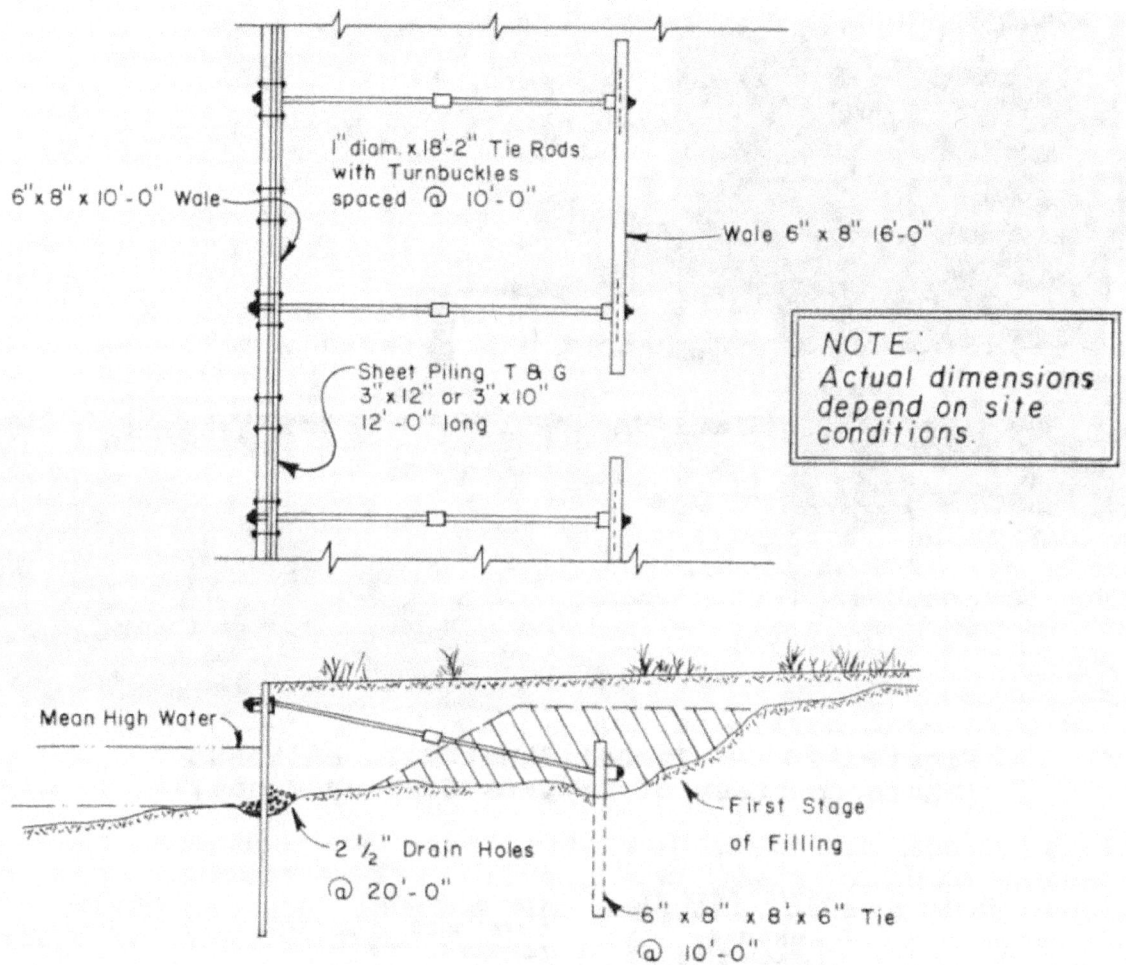

Figure 31. Plan View and Cross Section of Typical Sheet Pile Bulkhead [American Wood Preservers Institute (1970)]

Steel. Steel sheet piling, probably the most widely used bulkhead material (Figure 32), can be driven into hard, dense soil and soft rock. The interlocking feature of the sheet pile sections (Figure 33) provides a relatively sand-tight fit that generally precludes the need for filters. This close fit may also be essentially watertight, so regularly spaced weep holes are recommended. These, and lifting holes in the piling, should be backed with properly graded stone filters or filter fabric to prevent the loss of backfill.

Figure 32   Steel Sheet Pile Bulkhead

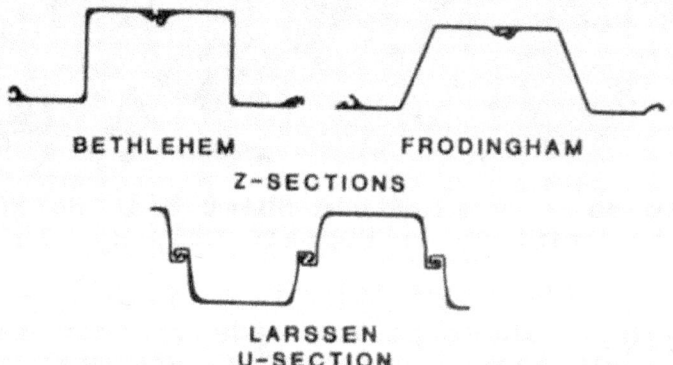

BETHLEHEM   FRODINGHAM
Z-SECTIONS

LARSSEN
U-SECTION

Figure 33   Steel Sheet Pile Sections
[After Winterkorn and Fang (1975)]

Aluminum.   Aluminum sheet pile sections are similar to steel.   Design and installation are accomplished using conventional methods and equipment. Its primary advantages over steel are lighter weight and superior corrosion resistance. Individual sheets can be carried and maneuvered by one man, and most drilling and cutting can be performed with simple hand tools. Its main disadvantage, compared to steel, is that it is less rugged when driven and cannot penetrate logs, rocks or other hard obstructions. Figure 34 is a Photograph of an aluminum bulkhead.

Figure 34   Aluminum Sheet Pile Bulkhead
(Photo Courtesy of Koppers Company, Inc.)

Asbestos-Cement.   Sheet piling made of this material has been tried in several locations. Indications are that it often suffers significant and rapid deterioration in a marine environment [Watson, Machemehl, and Barnes (1979)] and should be used with caution when long life is desired.

Post Supported Bulkheads

Post supported bulkheads consist of regularly spaced posts, usually timber, driven into the ground with an attached facing material that forms a retaining wall. The posts, support c6mponents of the bulkhead, resist the exerted earth pressures. As with sheet piling, a post supported bulkhead can be either a cantilever or anchored.

One advantage is that the posts can sometimes be installed using only an auger, and the facing material can then be placed by hand. The cost of the bulkhead depends on the required spacing of the posts, and the type of soil being augured.

Hogwire Fencing and Stacked Bags

Wave Height Range: Below five feet.

Hogwire fencing attached to posts can be used to support sand bags stacked on the landward side of the fence (Figure 35) to form a relatively inexpensive structure. The sand bags are vulnerable to tearing, however, if after being undercut by toe scour, they slide against the hogwire fencing.

Figure 35   Hogwire Fencing and Stacked Bag Bulkhead

For best performance, use small-mesh wire with a PVC coating, because bare wire fencing tends to cut the bags. Tearing of the front row of bags can be prevented by filling them with a sand cement mixture. Burlap bags can be substituted for the more expensive bags when a sand-cement mixture is used. The material and seams of all sand-filled bags must be resistant to ultraviolet light.

Place the bottom bags and fencing in a trench excavated to at least the depth of anticipated toe scour.   Anchor or brace the posts, or embed them deeply, allowing for loss of support because of toe scour. Provide adequate drainage of the retained embankment and place stone at the toe of the bulkhead.

Treated Timber

Wave Height Range: Below five feet.

Horizontal, pressure-treated planks can be spiked to the landward side of posts which are anchored to deadmen or piles in the backfill. The planks must be backed by filter cloth or graded stone to prevent soil losses through the cracks. Riprap toe protection should be provided (Figure 36).

Figure 36   Treated Timber Bulkhead

Untreated Logs

Wave Height Range: Below five feet.

Horizontal, untreated logs can be attached to the landward side of posts in areas like the Pacific Northwest where there is an abundance of such logs. The same precautions about adequate toe protection and filtering also apply. However, the large gaps between logs make adequate filter design more difficult. If a filter cloth is used, it should follow the log contours so that it is not excessively stressed by bridging large gaps. However, it is vulnerable to damage or vandalism, which would jeopardize the entire structure because of the resulting loss of retained fill.

Used Rubber Tires

Wave Height Range: Below five feet.

Used tires can be strung over two rows of treated posts set in a staggered pattern, with the tires abutting each other and filled with gravel (Figure 37). The posts can be tied back to logs buried in the backfill with filter cloth placed behind the tires before backfilling. Under wave action, the gravel tends to wash out of the tires, and the backfill can then escape. Although used tires can generally be obtained free, the cost of the structure is probably comparable to other bulkheads because of the required close post spacing.

Figure 37   Used Rubber Tire and Post Bulkhead

Railroad Ties and Steel H-Piles

Wave Height Range: Below five feet.

Steel H-piles can be driven at regular intervals and railroad ties placed between the flanges of adjacent piles to form a bulkhead (Figure 38). The toe of the structure should be protected by armor stone, and proper filtering and granular backfill are needed behind the structure. A 12-inch steel channel, welded to the top of the H-piles, serves to align the piles and retain the railroad ties. The structure has performed well and would be particularly useful where subsurface rock prevents driving sheet piling. However, its cost is probably higher than other effective devices.

Figure 38   Railroad Ties and Steel H-Pile Bulkhead

Miscellaneous Bulkheads

Longard Tubes

Wave Height Range: Below five feet.

A Longard tube is a patented, woven, polyethylene tube, filled with sand at installation (Figure 39) and available in 40- and 69-inch diameters, and lengths up to 328 feet. Like sand-filled bags, performance depends on the fabric remaining intact, and the tube completely filled. When filled, the tube is dense and heavy, yet flexible enough to settle if depressions occur. A properly installed Longard tube is placed on a woven filter-cloth extending 10 feet seaward of the tube. A small 10-inch tube, factory stitched to the seaward edge of the filter cloth, settles under wave action to provide toe protection.

The primary advantage of a Longard tube is the ease and speed with which it can be filled once equipment and materials are in place. Repairs are possible using sewn-on patches. The major disadvantage is its vulnerability to vandalism and damage by waterborne debris. A sand-epoxy coating can be applied to dry tubes after filling to provide significantly greater protection by deterring vandals and preventing puncture holes from enlarging. This coating cannot be applied to wet tubes. However, the tube must not be allowed to roll after the coating is applied, as uncoated surface areas would then be exposed, and distortion of the tube may cause the existing coating to flake off. other disadvantages are that a large supply of good quality sand is required to fill the tube, patented filling equipment must be used, and only specially licensed contractors can perform the work.

Figure 39   Longard Tube Bulkhead

The Longard tube depends on its weight to resist overturning and on friction to maintain its position. It is designed to protect the toe of the bank from wave attack, and not necessarily to resist earth pressures. The tube should not be placed directly against the base of a bank or overtopping waves may continue to cause erosion. It should be placed far enough from the toe so that overtopping waves will form a sand berm between the tube and the bank. Wave energy will be absorbed by this berm, and further bank erosion may be prevented. Placement of other devices or another tube on top, to increase the structure height and prevent overtopping, is not recommended.

Stacked Used Tires

Wave Height Range: Below two feet.

Because used tires are readily available at most sites at no cost, many have tried to use them for shoreline protection devices. The bulkhead on Figure 40 was made with scrap tires interconnected (both vertically and horizontally) by galvanized spikes and pushnuts. The tires were stacked in a staggered pattern over a filter cloth, and granular material was used both as backfill in low areas, and as fill in the tires. Three rows of galvanized steel anchors secured the structure to the beach. The structure progressively failed because the interconnections between the tires were inadequate to hold it together. The gravel washed out of the tires, eventually allowing them to be lifted by waves. This system is not recommended in view of better and less costly alternatives.

Figure 40   Stacked Used Tire Bulkhead

This structure illustrates a common problem with using scrap tires. While their availability is a strong temptation to use them in shore protection devices, tires are extremely rugged, and usually cannot be securely fastened together except by considerable labor and expense. In almost all cases, failure results because interconnections do not perform as expected.

Used Concrete Pipes

Wave Height Range: Below two feet.

This bulkhead is constructed by standing used concrete pipes on end, side-by-side, and then filling them with granular soil (Figure 41). This bulkhead is economical and practical only when there is an available supply of used concrete pipes and where a low structure is adequate.

A filter must be provided behind the structure to relieve hydrostatic pressures. If a filter cloth is used, it should be forced deeply into the grooves between pipes to avoid ballooning and bursting the cloth. The wall should not be more than two pipe diameters high without an anchoring system. Also, the pipes should be entrenched to provide stability and toe protection. A continuous concrete cap (not pictured) could be cast across the tops of all pipes to insure performance as a unit. This type of bulkhead may not last long because of possible rapid deterioration of the concrete pipes.

Figure 41   Used Concrete Pipe Bulkhead

REVETMENTS

The armor layer of a revetment maintains its position under wave action either through the weight or interlocking of the individual units.   Revetments may be classified as flexible, semi-rigid, or rigid. Flexible armors, such as quarrystone, riprap, or gabions, retain   their protective qualities even if the structure is severely distorted, such as when the underlying soil settles, or scour causes the toe of the revetment to sink. A semi-rigid armor layer, such as interlocking concrete blocks, can tolerate minor distortion, but the blocks may be displaced if they are moved too far to remain locked to the surrounding units. Once one unit is completely displaced, such revetments have little reserve strength and displacement will generally continue to complete failure. Rigid structures may be damaged and fail completely if subjected to differential settlement or the loss of support by underlying soil. Grout-filled mattresses of synthetic fabric and reinforced concrete slabs are examples of rigid structures.

Rubble

        Rubble revetments are constructed of one or more layers of stone, or concrete pieces derived from the demolition of sidewalks, streets and buildings. Stone revetments are constructed of either two or more layers of uniform-sized pieces (quarrystone), or a gradation of sizes between upper or lower limits (riprap). Riprap revetments are somewhat more difficult to design and inspect because of the required close control of allowable gradations and their tendency to be less stable under large waves. For that reason, graded riprap revetments should be used with caution, but they are acceptable for the majority of low cost shore protection applications. Quarrystone structures are more easily designed and inspected and are recommended.

The primary advantage of a rubble revetment is its flexibility, which allows it to settle into the underlying soil or experience minor damage and still continue to function. Because of its rough surface, it also experiences less wave runup and overtopping than a smooth-faced structure. The primary disadvantage is that placement of the stone or concrete armor material generally requires heavy equipment.

To insure good performance, prepare the existing ground to a stable slope. In most cases, the steepest recommended slope would be 1 vertical on 2 horizontal (1:2). Fill material should be added where needed to achieve a uniform slope, but it should be free of large stones and should be firmly compacted before revetment construction proceeds. Properly sized filter layers should be provided to prevent the loss of the slope material through voids in the revetment stone. If using filter cloth, an intermediate layer of smaller stone below the armor layer may help distribute the load and prevent rupture of the cloth.

No individual armor unit should be longer than three times its minimum dimension. In other words, avoid using plate-like or cylinder-shaped pieces; stones should be angular and blocky, not rounded. The toe of the revetment should be located one design wave height (but at least three feet) below the existing grade line to prevent undercutting in lieu of deep burial, a substantialsacrificial berm of additional rubble (with filtering) should be provided at the toe.

Quarrystone and Riprap

Wave Height Range: Above five feet (Quarrystone).

Below five feet (Riprap).

Stone revetments are a proven method of shoreline protection (Figure 42). They are durable and can be relatively inexpensive where there is a local source of suitable armor stone. Quarried stone should be clean, hard, dense , durable, and free of cracks and cleavages. Figure 43 shows a typical cross section of a stone revetment. The weight of the armor stones should be determined by the following formula as given in the Shore Protection Manual [U. S. Army Corps of Engineers (1977c)].

$$W = w_r H^3 / K_D(S_r - 1)^3 \cot \theta \qquad (17)$$

Where W = weight of an individual armor stone (pound);

W_r = unit weight (saturated surface dry) of the rock (lbs/ft^3)

H = wave height (feet);

S_r = specific gravity of the armor stone (w_r/w_w); where w_w = 64.0 lbs/ft^3 for salt water and 62.4

lbs/ft^3 for fresh water

$\cot \theta$ = slope of the structure expressed as horizontal units/vertical units

K_D = Stability coefficient from Table 12.

Table 12		
Stability Coefficients for Stone Revetments		
Armor Unit		
Quarrystone		
Smooth rounded		2.1
Rough angular		3.5
Graded riprap		2.2

Tables 13, 14 and 15 contain solutions for Equations 17 with an illustrative example of their use.

If uniform quarrystone is used, the individual stones should range from 0.75W to 1.25W with 75 percent of the stones weighing W or more. For graded riprap, W corresponds to W_{50} min and the recommended gradation is 3.6 W_{50}., to 0.22 W_{50}. Riprap should be limited to areas where the design wave height is less than five feet.

If a graded stone filter is employed, it may be significantly more fine-grained than the armor layer. This may require the use of an intermediate layer of stone between the armor and the filter. This layer should consist of units about 1/10 the weight of stone in the armor layer. This intermediate layer is also recommended wh6n a filter cloth is employed because it provides bedding and resists tearing or puncturing of the cloth under the heavy armor stone.

TABLE 13 ESTIMATED WEIGHT OF ARMOR STONE		TABLE 14 CORRECTION FOR SLOPE		TABLE 15 CORRECTION FOR UNIT WEIGHT	
WAVE HEIGHT H (ft)	ESTIMATED WEIGHT W (lb)	SLOPE (ft/ft)	CORRECTION FACTOR K_1	UNIT WEIGHT w_r (lb/ft^3)	CORRECTION FACTOR K_2
0.5	1	1 : 2	1.0	120	4.3
1.0	10	1 : 2½	0.8	130	2.8
1.5	20	1 : 3	0.7	135	2.4
2.0	50	1 : 3½	0.6	140	2.0
2.5	100	1 : 4	0.5	145	1.7
3.0	160	1 : 4½	0.4	150	1.5
3.5	260	1 : 5	0.4	155	1.3
4.0	390	1 : 5½	0.4	160	1.1
4.5	550	1 : 6	0.3	165	1.0
5.0	750			170	0.9
5.5	1000			175	0.8
6.0	1300			180	0.7
6.5	1650			185	0.6
7.0	2100			190	0.6

EXAMPLE

GIVEN: The wave height (H) is 3.0 feet and the structure slope is 1 on 3 (1 Vertical on 3 Horizontal) and one cubic foot of rock weighs 155 lbs (w_r)

FIND: The required weight of armor stone (W) from the tables (Dashed Line)

$$W = 160 \text{ lbs} \times 0.7 \times 1.3 = 145 \text{ lbs}$$

Concrete

Wave Height Range: Below five feet.

A concrete rubble revetment utilizes a waste product that is otherwise difficult to dispose of in an environmentally acceptable manner. The concrete should have the durability to resist abrasion by water-borne debris and ice pressure. In addition, all protruding reinforcing bars should be burned off prior to placement. Numerous concrete rubble revetments have failed in the past, but this has generally been attributable to neglect of filter requirements. Figure 44 shows two cross sections that would probably be more successful than random dumping on a slope. The upper section uses three layers of concrete rubble, shaped so that the longest dimension is no greater than three times the shortest, thus increasing stability and minimizing uplift on the slabs from wave forces. The revetment shown on Figure 45 is similar, except only one layer of rubble was used. It subsequently suffered damages, but more than one layer of rubble may have improved its performance. The lower section on Figure 44 utilizes shaped-rubble stacked on a slope to create a stepped face.

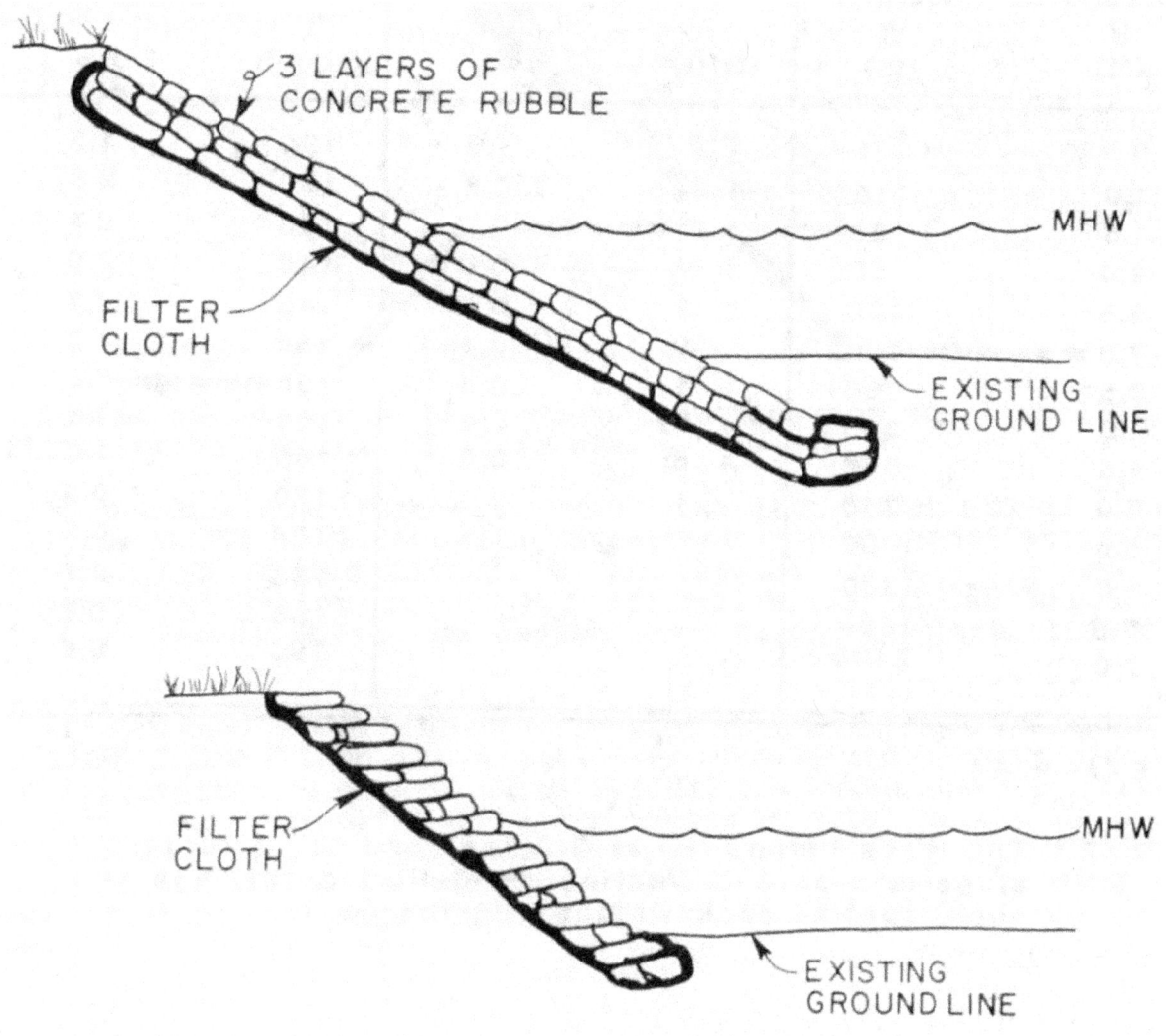

Figure 44   Concrete Rubble Revetment Sections

Concrete Blocks

Concrete blocks for semi-rigid armor layers are designed with various intermeshing or interlocking features, and many of the units are patented (Figure 46). Blocks have the advantage of neat, uniform appearance. Many units are light enough to be i stalled by hand once the slope has been prepared. The disadvantage of concrete blocks is that the interlocking feature between units must be maintained. Once one block is lost, other units so dislodge, and complete failure may result. A stable foundation required since settlement of the toe or subgrade can cause displacement of the units and ultimate failure. Also, some concrete block revetments have smooth faces that can lead to significantly higher wave runup and overtopping.

Figure 45   Concrete Rubble Revetment

Gobi (Erco) and Jumbo Blocks and Mats

Wave Height Range: Below five feet (blocks)
                   Above five feet (mats)

Gobi blocks are patented units that weight about 13 pounds each. Erco blocks are similar but they are offered by a different licensed manufacturer. Jumbo blocks are large-sized Erco Blocks that weigh about 105 pounds each. The units are designed hand-placement on a filter cloth or they are factory-glued carrier strip s of filter cloth. The latter are called Gobimats (Ercomats) or Jumbo Ercomats, depending on the size of the units If the blocks are glued to both sides of the carrier strip, backto-back, they are called double Gobimats (Ercomats) or double Jumbo Ercomats. Mats are preferred at sites where vandalism or theft is possibile. Both single and double mats require machine placement.

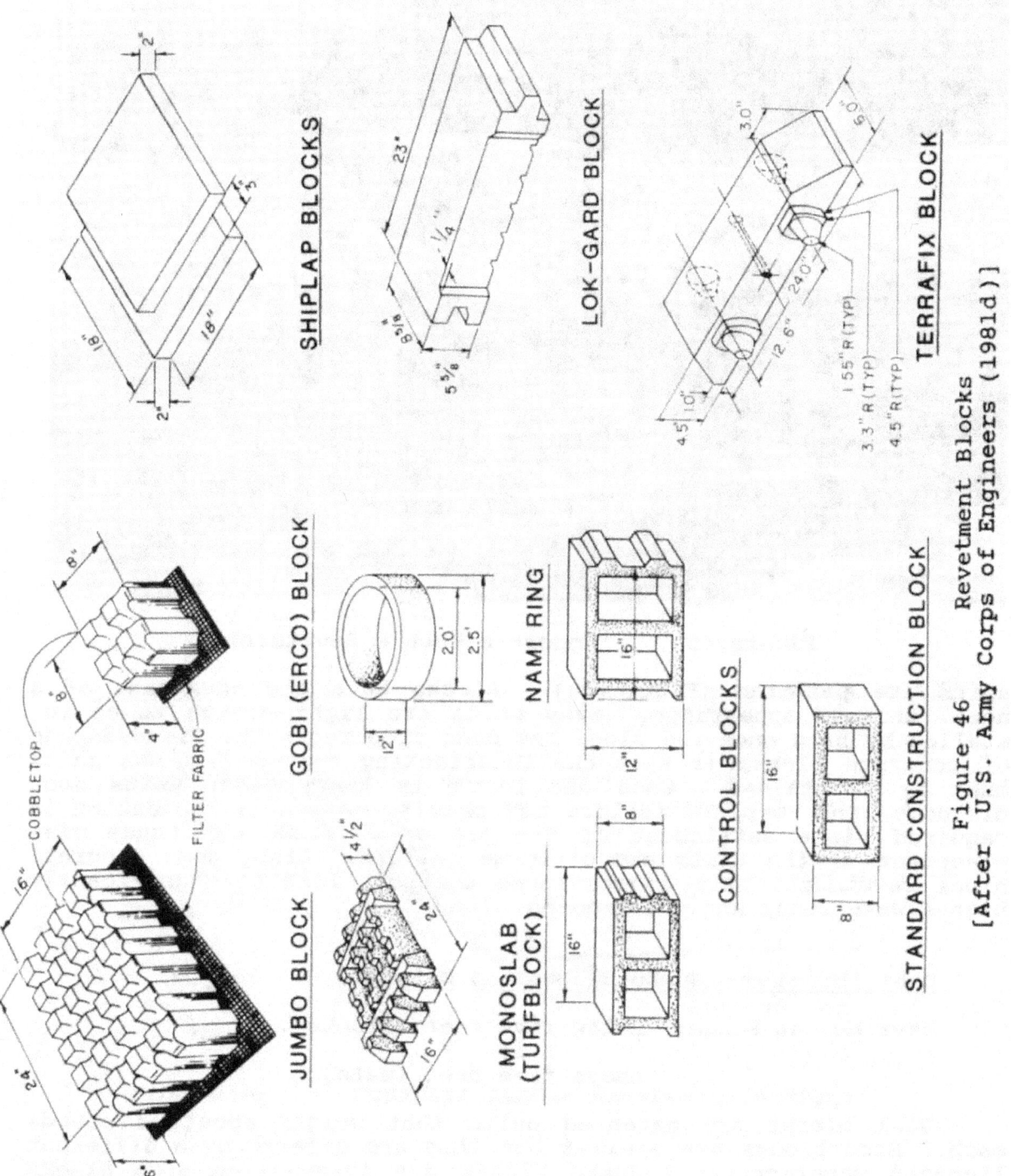

Figure 46   Revetment Blocks
[After U.S. Army Corps of Engineers (1981d)]

Block and mat revetments have generally performed well. A large project on the Gulf of Mexico in Louisiana has weathered several hurricanes and tropical storms with only moderate damage to the block sections and little or no damage to the mat portions. Figure 47 is a photograph of an existing revetment.

Figure 47   **Ercomat Revetment**

<u>Turfblocks or Monoslabs</u>.

Wave Height Range: Below five feet.

Turfblocks are designed for hand placement on a filter with the long axis parallel to the shoreline (Figure 48). Each block measures 16 x 24 x 4.5 inches and weighs approximately 100 pounds. Field installations have not yielded conclusive results, but their performance should be similar to Jumbo Erco blocks. Their thin, flat shape requires a stable foundation, as any differential settlement beneath the blocks makes them susceptible to overturning under wave action.

Figure 48   Turfblock Revetment

Nami Rings

Wave Height Range: Below five feet.

The Nami Ring is a patented concrete block shaped like a short section of concrete pipe, 2.5 feet in diameter by 1-foot high, and weighing 240 pounds. The rings are placed, side-by-side, on a slope over filter cloth. Better performance has been observed when the rings are joined together with tie rods. Sand or gravel caught up in the wave turbulence tends to be deposited inside the rings and in the voids between adjacent rings, adding to the stability of the section and protecting the filter cloth. Because of their shape, Nami Rings are susceptible to severe abrasion and damage by water-borne cobbles and, therefore, should be used primarily in sandy environments.

Control Blocks

Wave Height Range: Above five feet.

Control blocks come in various sizes and are similar to standard concrete construction blocks, except that protrusions in the block ends provide a tongue-and-groove interlock between units. Designed to be hand-placed on a filter cloth with. The cells vertical, the blocks can be aligned with their long axes parallel to shore, but optimum performance probably results from placement perpendicular to the water's edge (Figure 49).

Figure 49
Control Block Revetment

(Note: Perpendicular orientation of blocks with the waterline is preferred over the
parallel orientation shown in
this photograph.)

Concrete Masonry Blocks

Wave Height Range: Above five feet.

Standard construction masonry blocks should be hand-placed on a filter cloth with their long axes perpendicular to the shoreline and the hollows vertical. Their general availability is a primary advantage, but they are highly susceptible to theft. They form a deep, tightly fitting section which is stable provided the toe and flanks are adequately protected. Their primary disadvantage is that standard concrete for building construction is not sufficiently durable to provide more than a few years service in a marine environment. Special concrete mixes should be used when possible.

Shiplap Blocks

Wave Height Range: Below five feet.

Shiplap blocks are formed by joining standard concrete patio blocks with an epoxy adhesive. At 100 pounds or more per unit, they are designed for hand placement on a filter. The same precautions about concrete mixes apply here. These blocks are discussed in Hall and Jachowski (1964). A photograph and cross-section of one revetment are shown on Figures 50 and 51.

Figure 50   Shiplap Block Revetment

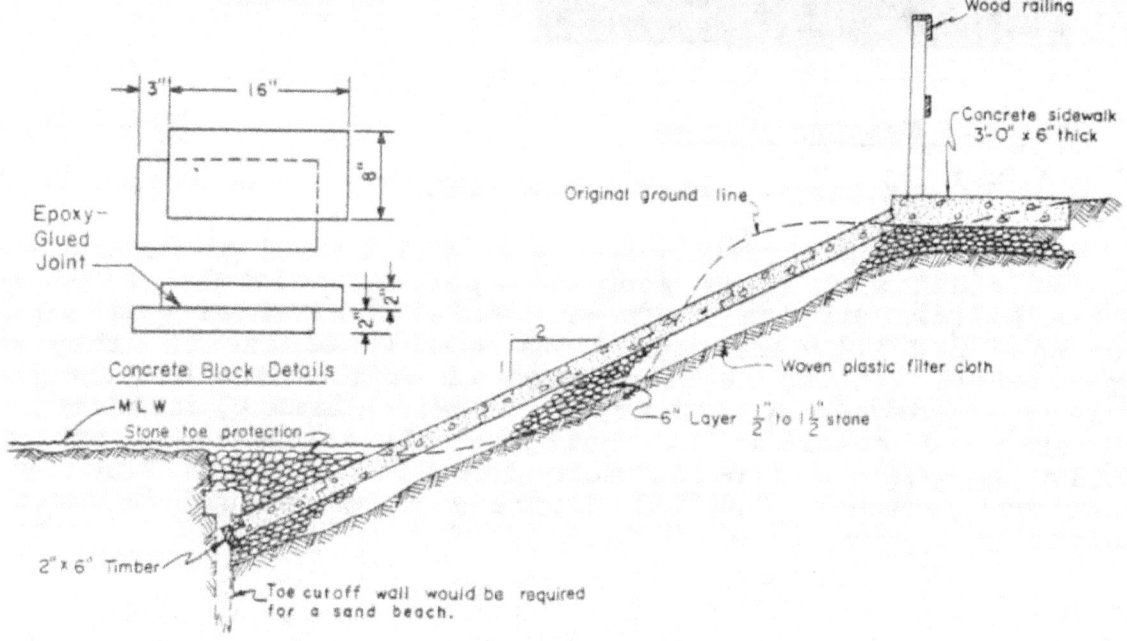

Figure 51   Shiplap Block Revetment Section
[U.S. Army Corps of Engineers (1977c)]

<u>Lok-Gard Blocks</u>

Wave Height Range: Below five feet.

Lok-Gard blocks join together using a tongue-and-groove system (Figure 52). The 80-pound, Patented units are designed to be hand-placed on a filter with their long axes perpendicular to the

Figure 52   Lok-Gard Block Revetment

Terrafix Blocks

Wave Height Range: Above five feet.

Terrafix blocks are patented units that join together with a mortise and tenon system, and have two cone-shaped projections, which fit holes in the bottom of the adjacent block (Figure 46). In addition, holes through the center of each block allow for stainless steel wire connection of many individual blocks. The uniform interlocking of the 50-pound units creates a neat, clean appearance (Figure 53).

Stacked Bags or Mats

Wave Height Range: Below five feet.

Several manufacturers produce bags and mats in various sizes and fabrics that are commonly filled with either sand or a lean mixture of concrete for use in revetments. While no special equipment is required for sand-filled units, a mixer, and possibly a pump, are needed for concrete-filled units. Bags should be filled and stacked against a prepared slope with their long axes parallel to the shoreline and joints offset as in brick work (Figure 54). Grout-filled bags can be further stabilized by steel rods driven through the bags.

Figure 53
Terrafix Block Revetment

(Photo Courtesy of Erosion
Control Products, Inc.)

The advantage of a bag revetment is its ease of construction and moderate cost. Sand-filled bags are relatively flexible and can be repaired if some of the original bags are dislodged. In addition, stacked bags are suitable as temporary emergency protection measures. Among their disadvantages, they are limited to low energy areas, have a relatively short service life compared to other revetments, and generally have an unattractive appearance. Since concrete-filled structures are rigid, any movement or distortion from differential settlement of the subgrade can cause a major failure that would be hard to repair. Sand-filled bags are highly susceptible to damage and possible failure from vandalism, impact by water-borne debris and deterioration of material and seams by sunlight. The smooth, rounded contours of bags also present an interlocking problem and they should be kept flatter and underfilled for stability.

Figure 54   Stacked Bag Revetment

Figure 55   Grout-Filled Mattress (Fabriform) Revetment
          (Photo Courtesy of Construction Techniques, Inc.)

Mattresses are designed to be laid flat on a prepared slope, joined together, and then filled (Figure 55).   They form a large mass of pillow-like concrete sections with regularly spaced filter meshes for the passage of water. They should always be installed according to the manufacturer's recommendations.

Bags or mattresses should be placed only on a stable slope. While a stacked bag revetment can be placed on a steeper slope than a mattress, it should not exceed 1 vertical on 1.5 horizontal. A stacked bag revetment should be at least two bags thick, preferably with the outside layer concrete-filled and the interior bags sandfilled. When sand is used as filler material, the bag or mat fabric, and its seams, must be resistant to ultraviolet light. Figure 56 shows a nonstabilized bag after six months of exposure. Where vandalism or water-borne debris are likely, only concrete-filled units should be used.

Figure 56   Deterioration of Sand Bags Under Ultraviolet Light

Some form of toe protection should be provided, or the toe should be buried well below the anticipated scour depth. Also, an adequate filter system, such as a properly installed and sized filter cloth, should be installed.

Some types of bags and mats which have been used in the past are described below.

Burlap Bags. Burlap bags are recommended only when filled with concrete because of rapid deterioration in the shoreline environment and the ease with which they can be torn.

Sand Pillows. Sand Pillows are ultraviolet-resistant bags made from a woven acrylic fabric. They weigh approximately 100 pounds when filled. Because of their resistance to sunlight, they are suitable for sand-filling in some areas.

Dura Bags. Dura Bags are large (4 x 12 x 1.7 feet), and must be filled in place using a pumped sand-slurry or concrete. Their large size makes them more resistant to movement under wave attack. Fabricated of ultraviolet-resistant material, they can be used in installations exposed to sunlight.

Fabriform Nylon Mat. The mat is designed to be filled with a highly fluid, lean-cement mixture. The exterior cloth envelope serves primarily as a form until the grout hardens. Fabriform is a patented product, available in several fabric styles, including some with filter points (weep holes) to provide slope drainage. Fabriform mats should be installed according to the manufacturer's instructions.

Miscellaneous

Gabions

Wave Height Range: Above five feet.

Gabions are rectangular baskets or mattresses made of galvanized, and sometimes PVC-coated, steel wire, in a hexagonal mesh (Figure 57). , Subdivided into approximately equal sized cells, standard gabion baskets are 3 feet wide, and available in lengths of 6, 9 and 12 feet and heights of 1, 1. 5 and 3 feet. Mattresses are either 9 or 12 inches thick. At the job site, the baskets are unfolded and assembled by lacing the edges together with steel wire. The individual baskets are then wired together and filled with 4- to 8-inch diameter stone. The lids are finally closed and laced to the baskets, forming a large, heavy mass (Figure 58).

Figure 57   Unassembled Gabions

Figure 58   Gabion Revetment

One advantage of a gabion structure is that it can be built without heavy equipment. Gabions are flexible and can maintain their function even if the foundation settles. They can be repaired by opening the baskets, refilling them, and then wiring the shut again.

The disadvantage of a gabion structure is that the baskets ma be opened by wave action. Also, since structural performance depends on the continuity of the wire mesh, abrasion and damage t the PVC coating can lead to rapid corrosion of the wire and failure of the baskets. For that reason, the baskets should be tightly packed to minimize movement of the interior stone and subsequent damage to the wire. Rusted and broken wire baskets also pose safety hazard. Gabion structures require periodic inspections s that repairs are made before serious damage occurs.

To insure best performance, use properly sized filler rock, interior liners or sandbags to contain smaller sized material are not recommended. The baskets should be filled tightly to prevent movement of the stone and they should be refilled as necessary to maintain tight packing.

Gabions should not be used where bombardment by water-born debris or cobbles is present, or where foot traffic across them is expected.

Steel Fuel Barrels

Wave Height Range: Below five feet.

This type of revetment is limited to remote areas with an abundance of used fuel barrels of little salvageable value (Figure 59). Due to rapid corrosion of the barrels in warm water, the system is only reliable in arctic regions. The barrels should be completely filled with coarse granular material to preclude damage by floe ice and debris, and the critical seaward barrels should be capped with concrete. Also, partial burial of the barrels increases stability.

Figure 59   Steel Fuel Barrel Revetment

Concrete Slabs

Wave Height Range: Below five feet.

Photographs of a typical structure were shown on Figure 20. The structure failed for a number of reasons, including improper filtering, inadequate toe protection, and lack of flank protection. Placed on a flatter slope, and with due regard for proper design considerations, this type of structure can provide low cost protection when large slabs are available.

Fabric and Ballast

Revetments using a fabric filter cloth as the slope's armor layer, held in place by some form of ballast, have not been successful And are not recommended.

BREAKWATERS

Breakwaters are either floating or fixed. Floating breakwaters function at or near the water's surface and must be firmly anchored to prevent displacement. Fixed breakwaters are constructed on the bottom and may or may not pierce the water's surface. When they do not, they are called sills. Their height and porosity determines how effectively they dissipate wave energy.

By trapping sand on their landward side, breakwaters protect the shore while simultaneously enhancing recreational uses. Unlike groins, they are able to trap sand moving both parallel and perpendicular to shore. Unfortunately, this sand-trapping (accreting) ability can also cause erosion of downdrift beaches. In most cases heavy construction equipment, often barge mounted, is necessary for breakwater construction.

Floating Breakwaters

Wave Height Range: Below five feet.

Floating breakwaters can be constructed of virtually any buoyant material such as rubber tires, logs, timbers, and hollow concrete modules. Floating breakwaters are particularly advantageous where offshore slopes are steep and fixed breakwaters would be expensive because of deep water. They can also be used where the tidal range is large and fixed breakwaters would be subjected to widely varying degrees of submergence. Floating breakwaters are also excellent for temporary installations, such as where vegetation requires protection while becoming established.

Floating breakwaters have several disadvantages as well. They are effective only against short-period waves (less than five seconds), which are those most commonly present in sheltered locations where low cost protection is most appropriate. Also, they may regarded as eyesores in some areas, they tend to collect floating debris, and they may require more maintenance than fixed breakwaters.

Rubber Tires. Two possible arrangements are shown on Figure 60. The upper configuration, known as a Wave-Maze, is patented and cannot be used without payment of royalties (See *Other Help* Section). The bottom configuration was developed by the Goodyear Tire and Rubber Company for promotional purposes and may be used without royalties. The use of other configurations is limited only by the imagination of the designer.

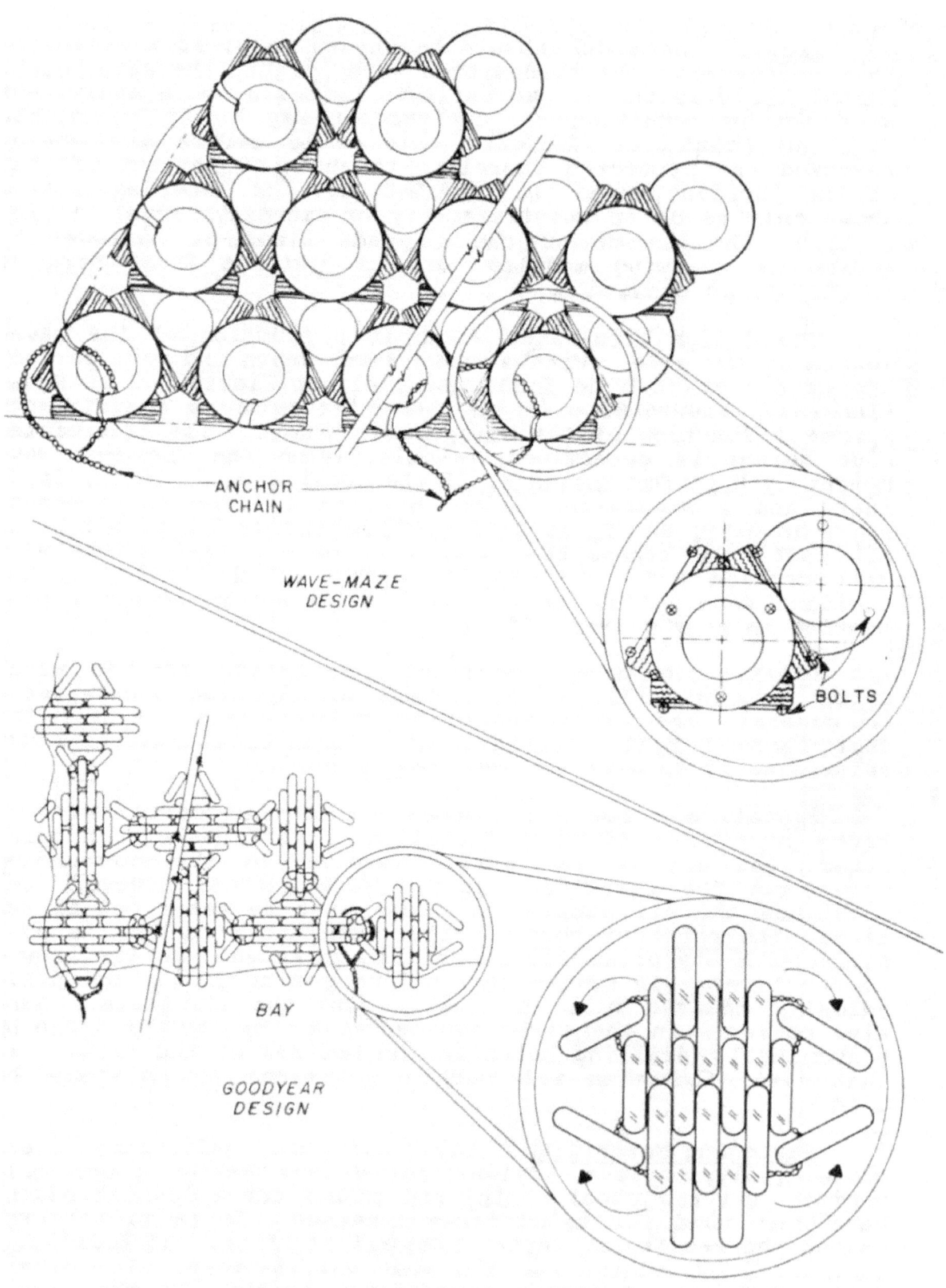

ANCHOR
CHAIN

WAVE-MAZE
DESIGN

BOLTS

BAY

GOODYEAR
DESIGN

Figure 60   Floating Tire Breakwater Modules
[After U.S. Army Corps of Engineers (1978b)]

The basic elements of design for floating tire breakwaters are listed below.

Length. The length parallel to shore should be sufficient to provide the desired protection and will vary with the structure's distance from shore.

Width. The width should be chosen to yield a satisfactory decrease in the transmitted wave height (the wave height behind the structure). No definite criteria would apply, but wave height reductions of 30 percent may be an acceptable starting point for design. This would reduce the energy reaching the protected shoreline to about 49 percent of that of the incident waves (0.7 x 0.7=0.49). If later experience shows this to be an unsatisfactory or excessive level of protection, the breakwater can be made wider or narrower by adding or removing modules, or its distance from shore or length can be changed.

The design breakwater width is a function of the wavelength at the site. with a known water depth and wave period, the wavelength can be found using either Figure 26, or Equation (3). Figure 61 gives the wave transmission coefficient, K as a function of the design wave height. The transmitted wave height is determined by multiplying the incident wave height by K. For instance, if the local wavelength, L, is 80 feet, and k breakwater width, W, of 40 feet is proposed, Wsh/L is 0.50, and K, is 0.90. If the incident wave height is 5 feet, the transmitted wave will be 4.5 feet. This wave will contain 0.9 x 0.9, or 81 percent of the energy of the incident wave. This may not be a satisfactory level of protection in many cases.

Draft. Increased depth of penetration in the water column increases the effectiveness of floating breakwaters. In general, the draft should be greater than one-half the design wave height. Two-layer structures or the use of truck or tractor tires will achieve greater draft.

Flotation. The air trapped within the top of vertical tires provides sufficient flotation in most cases. In quiet water, the air is eventually dissolved by the surrounding water and the structure sinks. Wave action, however, replenishes the air supply, but care must be taken not to use tires with puncture holes. More permanent flotation is possible with Styrofoam blocks or foam injected into the crowns of the tires. In salt water, marine growth that is not periodically removed will eventually sink the structure. Sand also collects in the tires and can sink them, but this can be prevented by drilling holes in the bottoms of the tires. In that case, flotation aids such as Styrofoam blocks should be used.

Fastening Materials. Stainless and galvanized steel cable; polypropylene, nylon, Poly-D and Kevlar rope; galvanized and raw steel chain; and rubber conveyor belt edging have been used for tying tires together. Davis (1977) presented the results of tests using all of these, and found that conveyor belt edging was the most satisfactory. The others failed because of either corrosion, abrasion by the tires, fatigue, or deterioration from other factors. Steel cables sawing through the tires have caused some devices to fail. Rubber belt edging, a scrap material derived from the manufacture of conveyor belts, is available from several rubber companies and comes in a wide range of widths and thicknesses. For tire breakwater construction, the belting should be at least 2 inches wide and 0.375 inches thick.

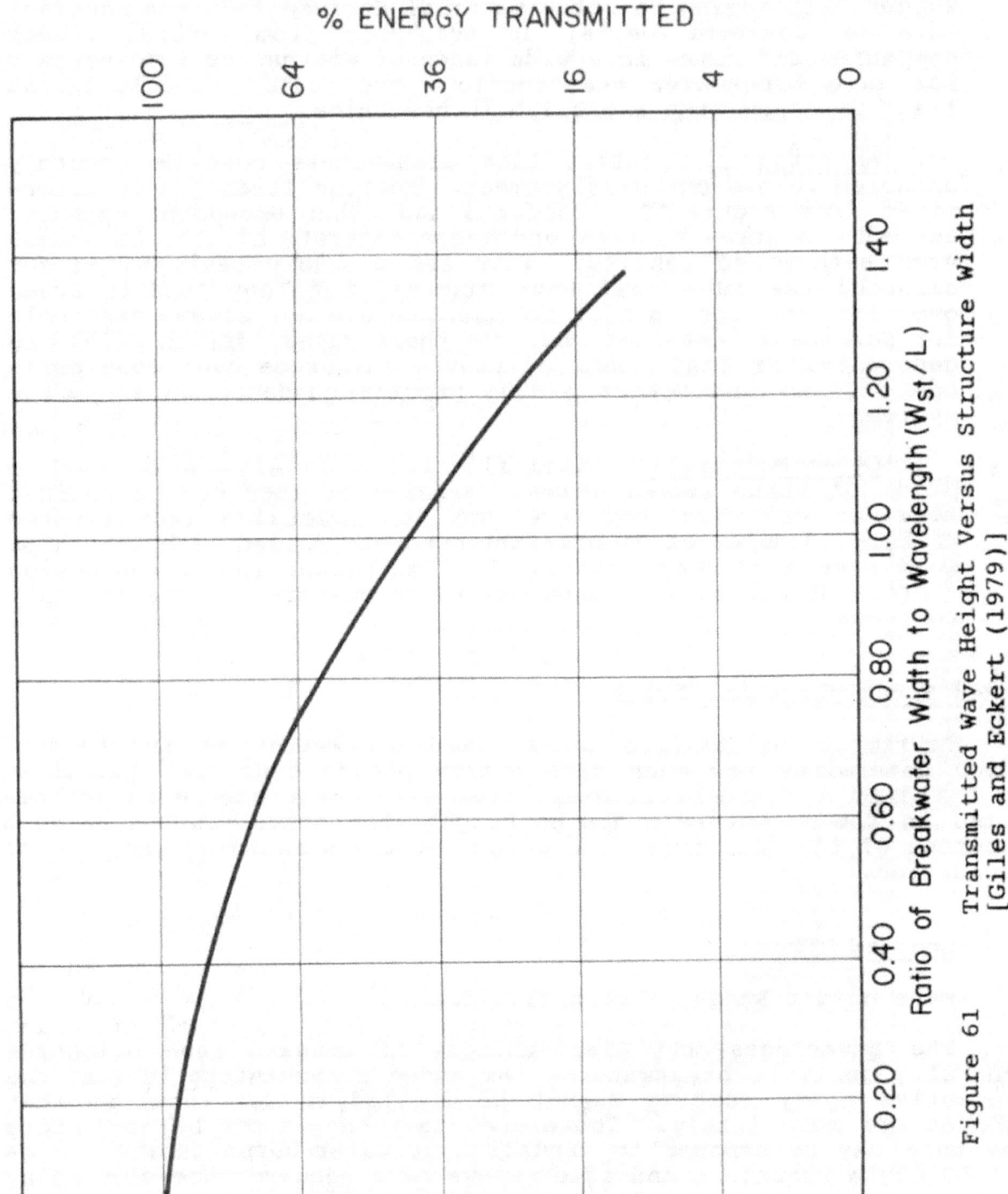

Figure 61   Transmitted Wave Height Versus Structure Width
[Giles and Eckert (1979)]

Anchorage. Floating tire breakwaters must be securely anchored to prevent displacement. Mooring loads can be determined from Figure 62. Danforth and other embedment anchors, as well as screw anchors and large concrete blocks, have been used with mixed results. They are probably best suited for seasonal use in a mild wave climate, but they tend to creep over long periods in soft bottoms and are not always desirable for permanent installations. In those cases, driven piles are generally the best means of stable anchorage over long periods. Giles and Eckert (1979) provide guidance on anchorage systems.

Other Materials. Other floating materials can be used in place of scrap rubber tires. Bundles of logs can be chained together or other barriers can be fabricated from treated timber. Modules of lightweight concrete filled with flotation foam have also been successful. The proportioning and design factors presented for rubber tire breakwaters would also apply to these.

Fixed Breakwaters and Sills

An important feature of a fixed breakwater is its height, which determines how much wave energy passes over the structure. In building a fixed breakwater, some settlement should be anticipated in the structure's design height, the actual amount being a function of the soil type, the weight of the structure, and type of foundation.

Longard Tubes

Wave Height Range: Below five feet.

The advantages and disadvantages of Longard tube bulkheads generally apply to breakwaters. An added disadvantage is that the protective epoxy coating cannot be applied to wet tubes so that damages are more likely. Therefore, they should not be used where the tube may be exposed to vandalism or water-borne debris. Figure 63 contains before and after views of a Longard tube slashed by vandals, eventually causing it to entirely deflate.

The tube should be installed over a layer of synthetic filtercloth with factory-sewn, 10-inch Longard tubes on each edge to reduce the potential for failure due to toe or heel scour. Where a 69-inch tube cannot provide sufficient height, an alternate breakwater system should be used.

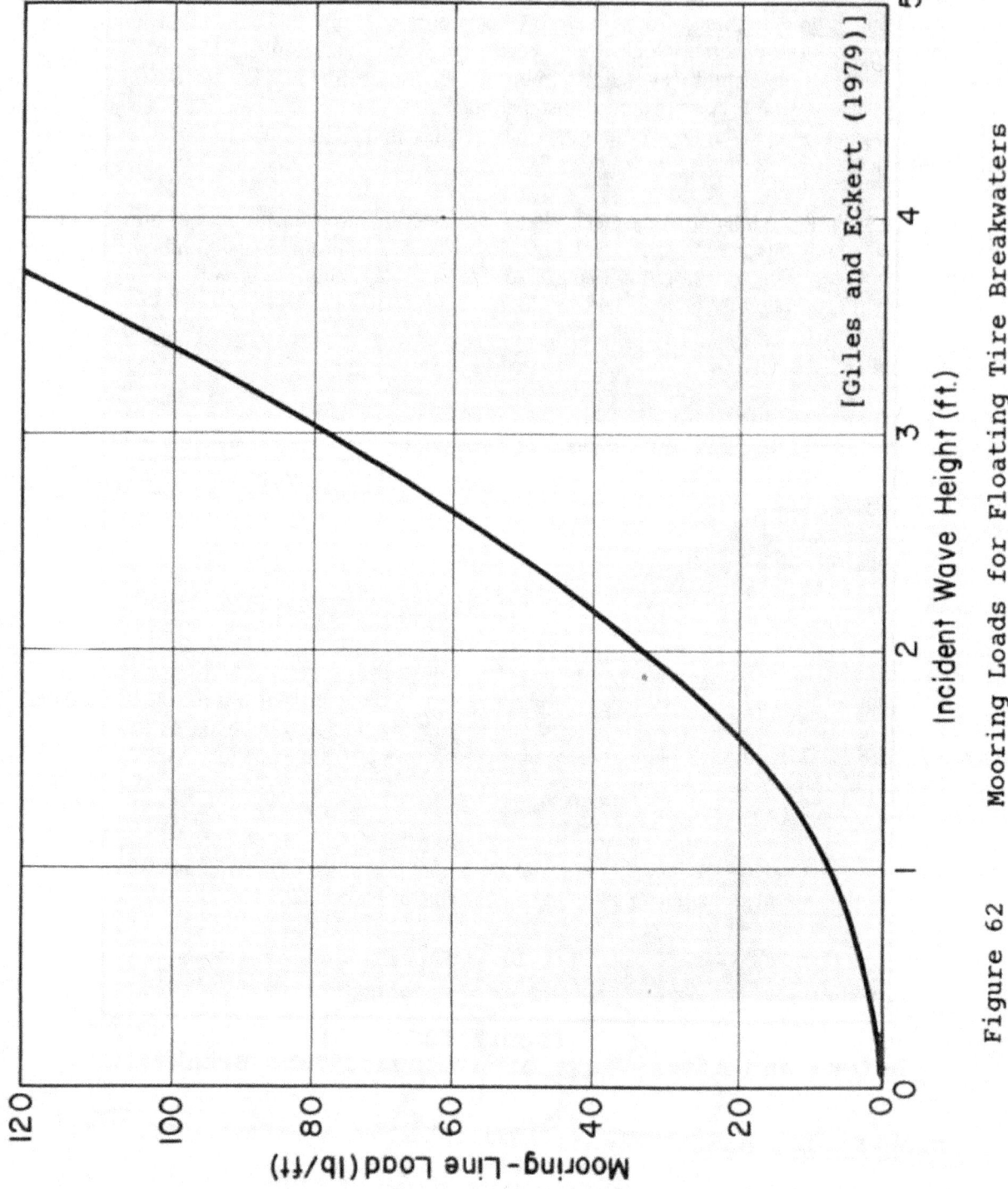

Figure 62   Mooring Loads for Floating Tire Breakwaters

[Giles and Eckert (1979)]

8 March 1979

15 November 1979

Figure 63
Before and After Views of a Longard Tube Breakwater

Sand-Filled Bags

Wave Height Range: Below five feet.

Sand-filled bag breakwaters are constructed of stacked bags in a staggered pattern (Figure 64). The integrity of the structure depends on the individual bags remaining in place and intact. T bags and seams must be resistant to ultraviolet light to preclude deterioration from prolonged sunlight exposure. They should not used where vandalism is expected or where the structure will exposed to water-borne debris. Lighter bags (100-pound range) like those used for revetments, are displaced when exposed to ev moderate waves. Larger units, such as Dura Bags, are recommend even through they are more difficult to handle and require filling in place.

Figure 64   Sand-Filled Bag Breakwater

A filter cloth should be placed under the bags to reduce settlement in soft bottoms (Figure 65). During construction bag-to-bag abutment should be insured to minimize wave transmission through gaps between bags.

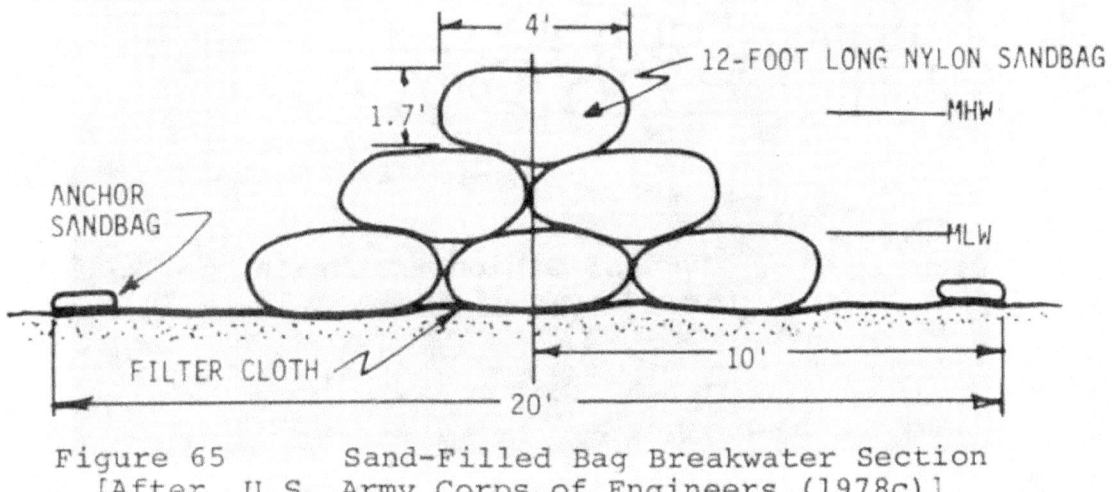

Figure 65   Sand-Filled Bag Breakwater Section
[After U.S. Army Corps of Engineers (1978c)]

Grout-Filled Bags

Wave Height Range: Below five feet.

The major advantage of grout-filled bags is that the units hold their shape after the fabric deteriorates or is torn. Again, use of larger bags is recommended because the smaller ones are susceptible to displacement. In addition, larger units reduce the number of bag contact points where openings may develop. The recommendations made for sand-filled bags also apply to grout-filled bags, except that vandalism is not a major concern.

Gabions

Wave Height Range: Below five feet.

The same basic design considerations for gabion revetments also hold here. The wire mesh should be PVC-coated, the baskets should be tightly packed, and a filter cloth should be used beneath the structure to help control settlement. A gabion mat should be provided around the structure to protect against scour. Tight packing of the stone is particularly important to avoid large distortion of the baskets under wave action. A typical cross section and photograph of a gabion breakwater are shown on Figures 66 and 67.

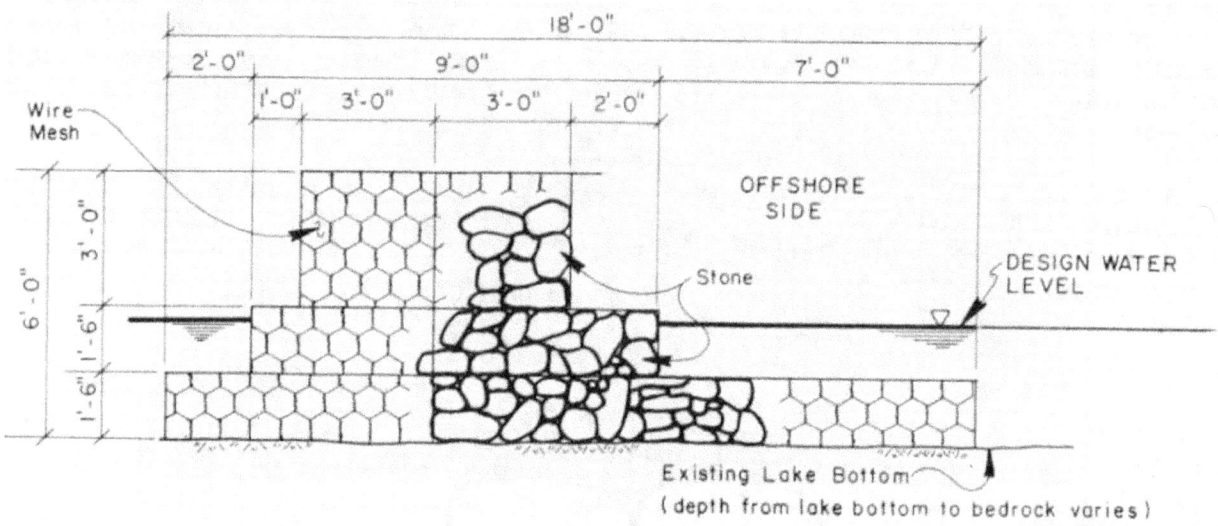

Figure 66   Typical Gabion Breakwater Section
[After U.S. Army Corps of Engineers (1978a)]

Figure 67   Gabion Breakwater

Z-Wall

Wave Height Range: Above five feet.

A Z-Wall is a patented device constructed with reinforced concrete panels set on edge in a zigzag fashion (Figure 68). The structure is designed for placement close to the shore on the existing bottom without the use of a filter. A single bolt acts a hinge that interconnects adjacent panels and allows for non-u form settlement, but with limited tolerance; so that Z-Walls sensitive to bottom conditions. If the tolerable differential settlement is exceeded, the panels tend to lean against or p apart from each other, causing the concrete to spall in stress areas. The nuts on the connecting bolts tend to unwind under w agitation, and should be inhibited by the use of double nuts destruction of the exposed threads behind the nuts. Otherwise, end units ma fall away if the nuts unwind completely.

Figure 68   Z-Wall Breakwater

The Z-Wall performs best at a site with a firm bottom. The six-foot panel height limits its use to relatively shallow water.

Surgebreaker

Wave Height Range: Above five feet.

A Surgebreaker is a modular device constructed with patented 3,700-pound, precast, reinforced concrete modules (Figure 69) with vent holes to release wave pressure buildup. The triangular modules are 4 feet high and 7 feet wide. They are designed to placed side-by-side on the existing bottom with the flatter slope face of the device toward the waves (Figure 70).

Figure 69   Surgebreaker Modules

Figure 70   Surgebreaker Breakwater

Sandgrabber

Wave Height Range: Below five feet.

A patented configuration of interconnected concrete construction blocks (Figure 71), the Sandgrabber is a device that allows for some differential settlement of the blocks by using U-shaped, galvanized-steel connecting rods. The hollow blocks allow waves to wash sand through, trapping the coarser, water-borne particles behind the structure. The Sandgrabber must be installed by a franchised contractor.

Figure 71   Sandgrabber

The current design does not use any form of toe protection, nor is the structure placed on a filter. As a result, the structure normally settles unevenly and rotates seaward into a scour trench. Because of these movements, the allowable amount of differential settlement is sometimes exceeded and the resulting stress of the U-ties against the concrete blocks may crack or break them. This can eventually lead to complete collapse of the structure. Weak Concrete hastens the process, so compressive strength tests should be performed on each batch of blocks before construction. A precaution when using a Sandgrabber, or any other breakwater, is to avoid downdrift erosion damages. Backfilling with sand should prevent any potential problems.

Quarrystone

Wave Height Range: Above five feet.

A stone breakwater is structurally similar to a stone revetment (Figure 72) and stone sizes should also be selected by using Equation (17). However, the stability coefficient, KD, should be selected from Table 16, rather than Table 12.

Table 16

Figure 72   Quarrystone Breakwater

Armor	Layers	Structure Trunk K_D	Structure Head (End) K_D	Slope cot 0
Table 16				
KD VALUES FOR STONE BREAKWATERS				
Quarrystone Smooth rounded	2	2.1	1.7	1.5 to 3.0
Rough angular	2	3.5	2.9	1.5
			2.5	2.0
			2.0	3.0
Graded riprap		Not Recommended		

A major advantage of a quarrystone breakwater is that the structure does not necessarily fail when differential settlement occurs. Through the years, stone has been used for more breakwater construction than any other material. It is time-tested and can be quite economical if suitable rock is available locally.

Timber Piles and Brush

Wave Height Range: Below two feet.

A brush breakwater is constructed of two parallel rows of posts driven into the offshore bottom, connected across the top with timber crossties, and filled with brush. Brush should be cut longer than the space between the posts and placed parallel to the structure alignment. Not suitable for permanent protection, this breakwater can be used for temporary sheltering of young vegetation.

Used Tires and Timber Piles.

Wave Height Range: Below two feet.

Timber piles can be driven into the bottom, so that every three piles form a triangular pattern, and used automobile tires can then be stacked on the piles. Just above the top tires, the triangularly grouped piles should be interconnected using 2 x 6inch planks bolted to the piles (Figure 73). The structure, whose stability depends on the depth of pile penetration, has proven effective against mild wave action.

Figure 73   Used Tire and Timber Pile Breakwater

GROINS

Important design considerations for groins include their height, length, spacing (if there are more than one) and the littoral transport rate. Their height determines how much sand can pass over the structure. Low groins, which essentially follow a foot or two above the natural beach profile, are widely used because they stabilize the beach but do not trap excessive amounts of sand and thereby cause downdrift damages. The groin length should not extend past the breaker zone or else it may force the bypassing sand too far offshore and cause downdrift erosion damages. The groin spacing should generally be two or three times the groin length.

Groins can be built as sheet pile structures that depend on ground penetration for support, or as gravity structures that resist movement solely because of their weight. In-either case, it is essential to prevent or adequately plan for bottom scour. For sheet pile structures, scour reduces their amount of embedment and makes them vulnerable to tipping. Rigid gravity structures can settle unevenly and be damaged if undermined by scour.

Stacked Baqs

Wave Height Range: Below five feet.

A stacked bag groin is similar to a stacked bag breakwater (Figure 74). The bags can either be sand or grout-filled. As with breakwaters, larger bags are recommended because lighter, smaller bags are too susceptible to displacement. The recommendations for bag breakwaters also apply to groins. The bags in the photo were filled between wooden forms to achieve their blocky shape, but this was unnecessary. When installed properly, stacked bag groins have performed well; however, they should only be considered a short-term solution when filled with sand.

Figure 74   Stacked Bag Groin

Gabions

Wave Height Range: Above five feet.

The recommendations for gabion revetments generally apply. The groin should be underlain with filter cloth to inhibit settlement, and all baskets should be made from PVC-coated wire mesh. Tiers of baskets should be tied together with appropriately sized wire to prevent shifting of upper tiers over lower tiers, and tight packing is needed to minimize distortion of the baskets and damage to the wire. Adequate toe protection is required to prevent settlement and basket distortion. Thin gabion mattresses are ideal for this purpose.

Figure 75 shows a gabion groin.

Figure 75   Gabion Groin

Steel Fuel Barrels

Wave Height Range: Below five feet.

The use of steel fuel barrels for construction is only economical in remote arctic areas where used barrels are readily available and they have no other salvage value. Barrel groins have worked well where littoral transport characteristics are suitable for shore stabilization with a low groin. The barrels should be completely filled with gravel to protect them from crushing by ice floes or from damage due to floating debris. They should also be capped with concrete for additional strength, and entrenched to prevent undermining by scour on the downdrift side.

Quarrystone

Wave Height Range: Above five feet.

Quarrystone, a durable and time-tested material for shore protection, should always be considered where locally available. Figure 76 contains a typical cross section and profile of a quarrystone groin. The stone should be sized using Equation (17) and values from Table 16. Figure 77 is a photograph of a quarrystone groin.

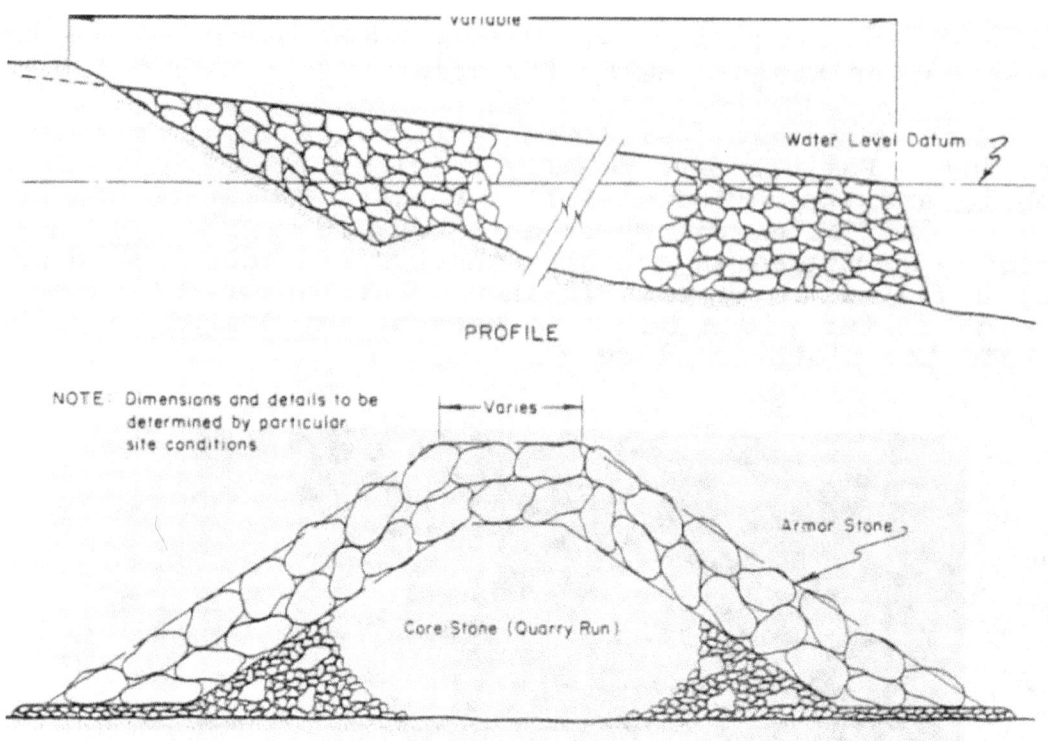

Variable

Water Level Datum

PROFILE

NOTE: Dimensions and details to be determined by particular site conditions

Varies

Armor Stone

Core Stone (Quarry Run)

CROSS-SECTION

Figure 76   Quarrystone Groin Section and Profile [U.S. Army Corps of Engineers (1977c)]

Figure 77   Quarrystone Groin

Longard Tubes

Wave Height Range: Below five feet.

Longard tubes have performed fairly well when remaining intact (Figure 78). Failure has usually resulted from holes or tears in the fabric and loss of sand fill. Longard tubes are probably best as a short term or emergency measure because of their vulnerability to damage. When used as a groin, the Longard tube should be underlain by a filter cloth with 10-inch tubes factory-stitched to each side. The filter cloth helps to prevent settlement, and the small tubes hold the cloth in place.

Figure 78   Longard Tube Groin

Sheet Piling

Wave Height Range: Above five feet.

Sheet pile groins, an old and proven means of shore protection, can be constructed of timber, steel, or aluminum sheeting. Toe protection or adequate embedment is required to insure the structure's stability. The general recommendations given for sheet pile bulkheads also apply to groins. Figure 79 contains a section and profile, and Figure 80 a photograph of a typical sheet pile groin.

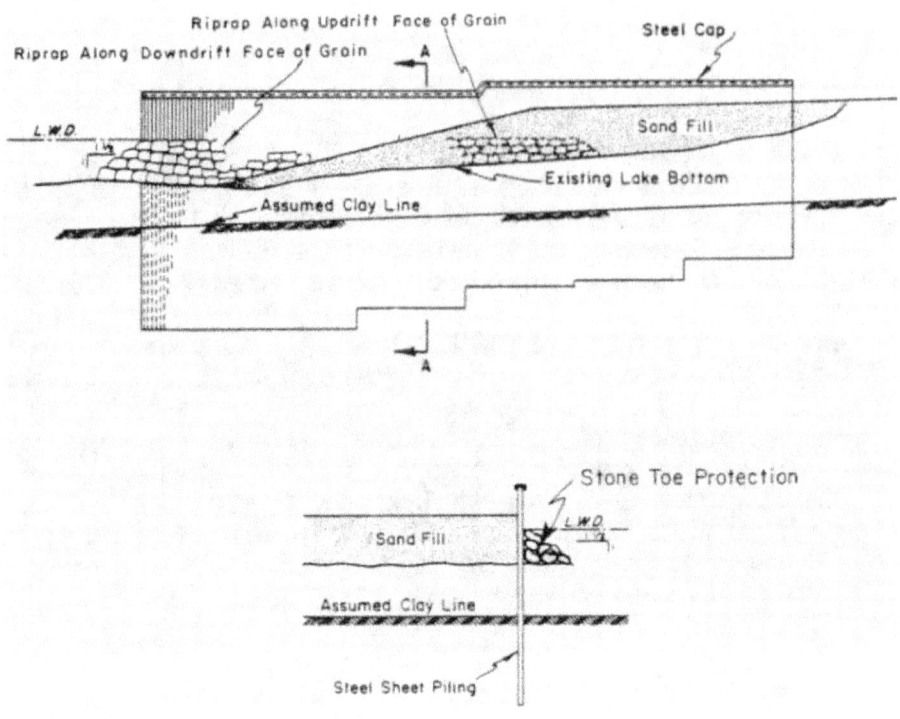

SECTION A-A

Figure 79   Sheet Pile Groin Section
[U.S. Army Corps of Engineers (1977c)]

Figure 80   Timber Sheet Pile Groin

Timber and Rock

Wave Height Range: Below five feet.

Many structural forms are possible for timber and rock groins. Figure 81 shows a timber crib structure that retains a stone f ill. Care must be taken to   insure that the rock is larger than the gaps between the timbers. Rock has escaped from the offshore compartment of the groin in the figure for that reason. Treated timbers should be used; and to insure structural stability, they should be securely fastened together with long wrought iron or coated steel rods, threaded at the ends to accommodate washers and nuts.

Alternate arrangements for timber groins are possible. Two rows of round structural piles can be driven or augured deep into the beach, with timber planking spiked to the piles. The piles can be placed close together with the planking set in the space between (Figure 82), or the piles can be more widely separated to form a crib-type structure (Figure 83).

Figure 81   Timber Crib Groin

Figure 82   Timber Plank Groin

Figure 83   Timber Plank Groin

BEACH FILLS

Beach fills are constructed by mechanical means such as dredging and pumping from of f shore deposits, or by overland hauling and dumping by trucks. The resulting beach provides some protection to the area behind it, while also serving as a valuable recreational resource.

An excess of fill will have to be placed initially because the finer material will be lost from the beach as the waves sort the deposit. The amount of overfill needed to account for these initial losses depends on the textural characteristics of the fill and the in-place material. These are compared by using measures of the mean grain size and sorting of the sand samples as given by Hobson (1977). Sorting is an indication of the range of particle sizes that are present. A *well sorted* sample contains particles that are' approximately the same size. A *poorly sorted* sample contains a gradation of particle sizes.

Mean grain sizes and sorting are expressed in phi units. These are defined as,

$$\phi = -\log_2 d_{(mm)} \qquad (18)$$

where, $d_{(mm)}$ = the particle diameter in millimeters. Note,

$$\log_2 d_{(mm)} = \log_{10} d_{(mm)} / \log_{10}(2).$$

Therefore

$$\phi = -3.32 \log_{10} d_{(mm)} \qquad (19)$$

Table 17 compares the millimeter and phi size scales.

Table 17

PHI VERSUS MILLIMETER PARTICLE SIZES

$D_{(mm)}$	ϕ
256	-8
64	-6
8	-3
4	-2
2	-1
1	0
0.5	1
0.25	2
0.125	3
0.0625	4

An estimate of the mean particle size is

$$M = (\phi_{84} + \phi_{16})/2 \qquad (20)$$

Where ϕ_{84} and ϕ_{16} are points on the gradation curve than represent the percentage of the sample that is coarser than the particular phi size. Phi sorting can be estimated by

$$S = (\phi_{84} - \phi_{16})/2 \qquad (21)$$

Figure 84 provides a fill factor that specifies the amount of fill material needed to produce a given volume of in-place material. The axes are defined in terms of the mean particle size of the borrow (fill) and native (in-place) material (M_b, and M_n), and the sorting of the borrow and native material (S_b, and S_n). For instance, if M_b, = 3.0, S_b, = 2.0, M_n = 3.50 and S_n = 1.00; the fill factor from figure 84 is 1.2. Therefore, if a beach containing 1,000 cubic yards of sand is desired, it will be necessary to initially place about 1,200 cubic yards of sand from the borrow source.

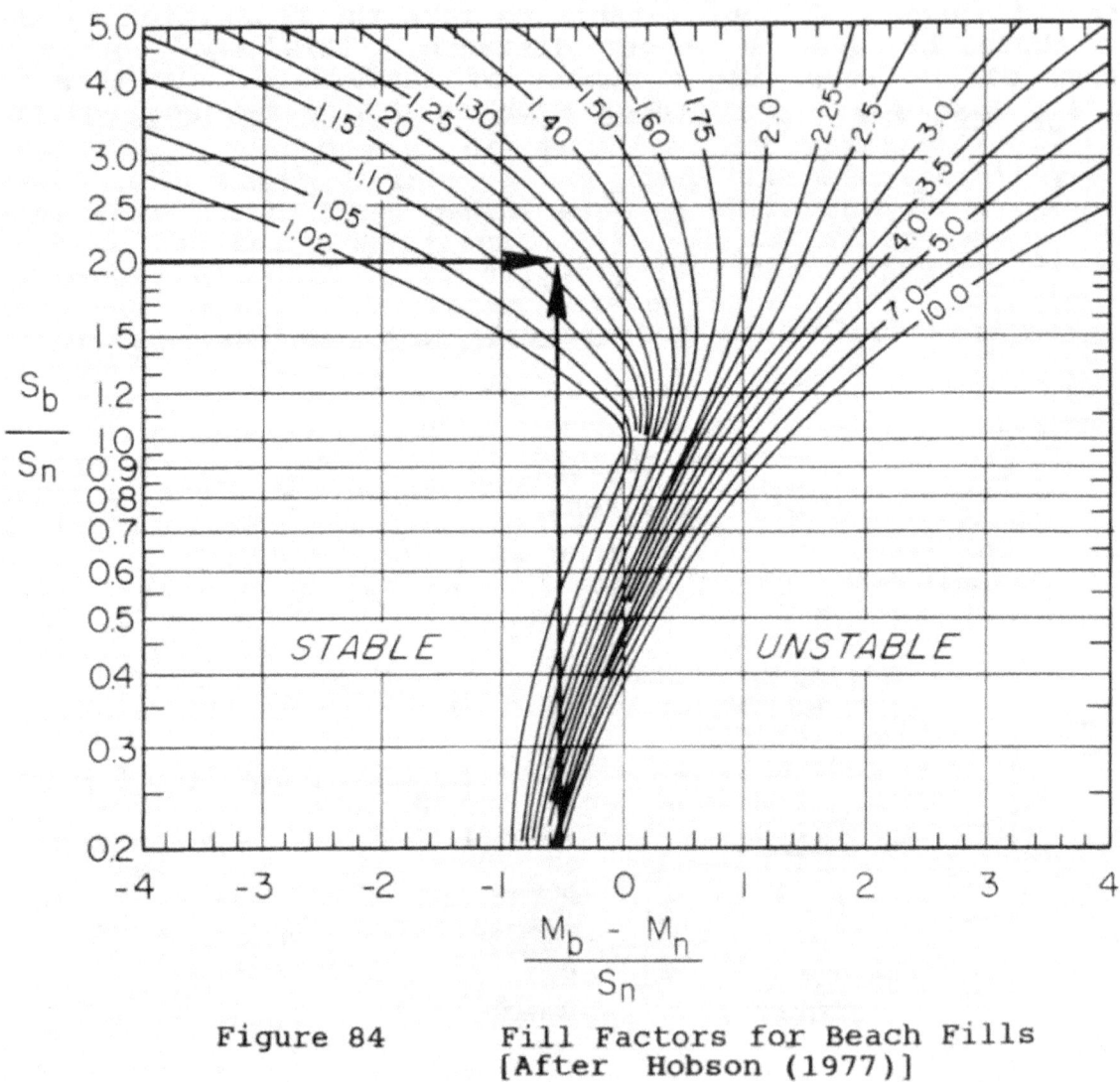

Figure 84   Fill Factors for Beach Fills
[After Hobson (1977)]

Figure 85 illustrates the important design factors to consider when constructing a beach fill. The berm elevation should be chosen to decrease the likelihood of overtopping by waves during storms. The berm width is determined by geometry to provide for the volume of fill to be placed, or for the shoreline use requirements. The beach slope should be chosen to parallel the existing profiles and slopes. This is based on the assumption that the existing beach is in equilibrium with the wave forces and that the new beach will eventually assume a similar shape. The shaping of the beach fill profile can either be done by equipment at the time it is placed, or it can be reshaped by waves. The final equilibrium slope will depend on the texture of the fill material, coarser-grained sand resulting in a steeper beach slope than previously existed.

If fill is placed over a short length of shoreline, it will create a projection that will be subject to increased wave attack. Therefore, it is generally preferable to make the transition to the existing shoreline over a longer distance. This may require a cooperative effort involving a number of landowners. If this is impractical, protective structures such as groins may be required to retain the fill.

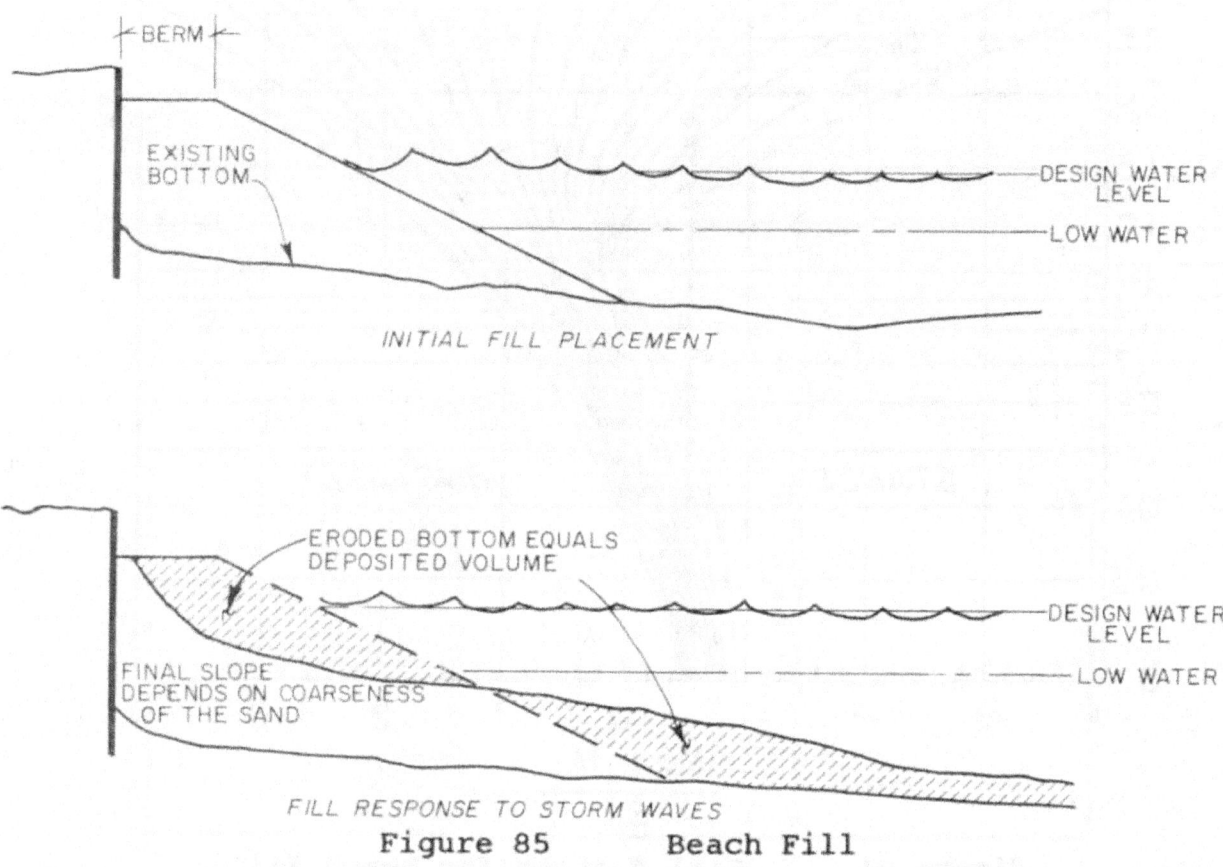

Figure 85   Beach Fill

VEGETATION

Vegetation has been used for stabilizing shorelines either as a substitute for, or supplement to, structures. Vegetation is an inexpensive, and generally easy, approach to providing erosion control.
It is not, however, applicable to all situations. It cannot always prevent erosion, nor can it stop the recession of bluffs caused by groundwater seepage. In order to confront these types of problems, it is necessary to consider a combination solution such as a structural device and vegetation.

Vegetation uses are limited by site characteristics such as climate, soil properties, wave exposure, and salinity regimes. The following discussion will focus on species which may be used for marsh, beach, dune and slope plantings. For each species, the applicable geographical region and planting specifications will be described. Further information on these and other species not mentioned in this report can be obtained from county offices of the Soil Conservation Service, state coastal zone management programs, or Corps of Engineers districts.

Marsh Plants

Coastal marshes are those herbaceous plant communities, which are normally inundated or saturated by surface or groundwater. They may be narrow fringes along steep shorelines or they may cover wide areas in shallow, gently sloping shore regions typically found in bays and estuaries (Figure 86). In saltwater marshes, salinity is generally equal to or slightly less than seawater (35 parts per thousand salt). Freshwater marshes experience water level fluctuations resulting from groundwater table and seasonal climatic changes.

To establish a coastal marsh, the site must be evaluated based on geographic area, tidal elevation and range, salinity, fetch length, and soil properties. The vegetation prevalent in three saltwater marsh regions and the Great Lakes are discussed below. Planting specifications are summarized in Table 18. The suitability of a site for marsh plantings can be evaluated using Figure 87.

Atlantic Coast Marshes. Common vegetation found in Atlantic coast marshes is described briefly below.

Smooth Cordgrass *(Spartina alternaflora)*. This is the dominant marsh grass from Newfoundland to about central Florida. It is well adapted to soils not exposed to air that range from coarse sands to silty clays. Three distinct height forms are recognized. The tall form is generally found along tidal creeks and drainage channels, the short form grows on flat or gently sloping areas away from channels, and the medium form, when present, is found in transition areas between stands of the short and tall forms.

Table 18

PLANTING SPECIFICATIONS FOR MARSH PLANTS

Type	Planting Time	Plant Form Recommended	Spacing	Tidal Range and Plant Location
Atlantic Coast Marshes				
Smooth cordgrass (*Spartina alterniflora*)	March-May	Sprigs 15 week old seedlings 6 month old seedlings or plugs	3' apart 1.5' apart 1.5' apart	< 4.5' range-plant MLW to MHW > 4.5' range-plant MTL to MHW
Saltmeadow cordgrass (*Spartina patens*)	March-May	Sprigs 15 week old seedlings	3' apart	MHW to estimated highest tide
Black needle rush (*Juncus roemerianus*)	Spring	Seedlings	As 1-5 percent of cordgrass plantings	Above MHW
Common reed (*Phragmites communis*)	Spring	Sprigs	1.5'-3.0' apart	Above MHW
Mangroves Black (*Avicennia germinans*) Red (*Rhizophara mangle*) White (*Laguncularia racemosa*)	Late February-March	Seedlings Established plants	1.5' apart 6'-10' apart	Generally MTL and above
Gulf Coast Marshes				
Gulf cordgrass (*Spartina spartinae*)	March-May	Sprigs 15 week old seedlings 6 month old seedlings	1.5'-3.0' apart 1.5' apart 1.5' apart	MHW and above
Saltgrass (*Distichlis spicata*)	Spring	Seedlings	1.5'-3.0' apart	MHW and above
Pacific Coast Marshes				
Pacific cordgrass (*Spartina foliosa*)	April	Sprigs	1.5'-3.0' apart	Below MTL
Pickleweed (*Salicornia spp.*)	Spring	Sprigs Seeds	0.5'-3.0' apart 5-10 seeds/sq ft	MHW to estimated highest tide
Sedge (*Carex lyngbyei*)	April-June	Seedlings	1.4'-3.0' apart	Above MTL
Tufted hair grass (*Deschampsia caespitosa*)	April-May	Seedlings	1.5'-3.0' apart	Above MLHW
Arrowgrass (*Triglochlin maritima*)	April-June	Seedlings	1.5'-3.0' apart	Above MTL

Figure 86   Marsh Vegetation

Smooth cordgrass can be planted with a better chance of success than any other coastal marsh species native to the United States. Its ideal salinity range is 10 to 35 parts per thousand. Two to four weeks after planting, 30 to 45 lb/ac of a fertilizer which contains equal parts of available nitrogen and phosphate should be applied.

Saltmeadow Cordgrass *(Spartina patens)*. This species is extensive in the irregularly flooded high marsh zone along the Atlantic coast. It is able to withstand extended periods of both flooding and drought, growing in spots where the surface drainage is poor and water ponds during rainy periods. It cannot, however, tolerate the daily flooding of the intertidal zone. Saltmeadow cordgrass is a valuable stabilizer in the zone between smooth cordgrass and the upland grass species.

Two to four weeks after planting, 30 to 45 lb/ac of fertilizer containing equal parts of nitrogen and phosphate should be applied.

1. SHORE VARIABLES	2. DESCRIPTIVE CATEGORIES (SCORE AS INDICATED)						3. SCORE
a. FETCH - AVERAGE AVERAGE DISTANCE IN KILOMETERS (MILES) OF OPEN WATER MEASURED PERPENDICULAR TO THE SHORE AND 45° EITHER SIDE OF PERPENDICULAR 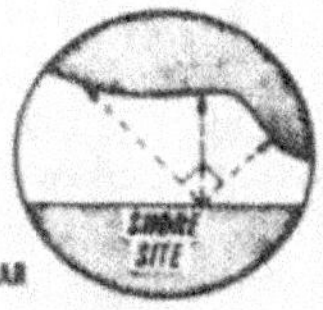	Score: 0 — LESS THAN 3.0 (1.8)	Score: 2 — 3.1 (1.9) to 6.0 (3.7)	Score: 4 — 6.1 (3.8) to 9.0 (5.6)	Score: 6 — 9.1 (5.7) to 12.0 (7.5)	Score: 8 — 12.1 (7.6) to 15.0 (9.4)	Score: 10 — GREATER THAN 15.0 (9.4)	
b. FETCH - LONGEST LONGEST DISTANCE IN KILOMETERS (MILES) OF OPEN WATER MEASURED PERPENDICULAR TO THE SHORE OR 45° EITHER SIDE OF PERPENDICULAR 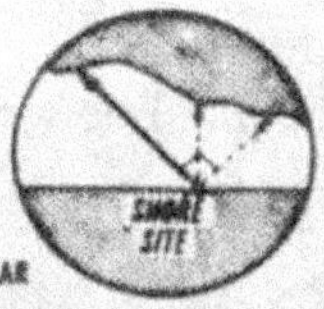	Score: 0 — LESS THAN 4.0 (2.5)	Score: 2 — 4.1 (2.6) to 8.0 (5.0)	Score: 4 — 8.1 (5.1) to 12.0 (7.5)	Score: 6 — 12.1 (7.6) to 16.0 (10.0)	Score: 8 — 16.1 (10.1) to 20.0 (12.6)	Score: 10 — GREATER THAN 20.0 (12.6)	
c. SHORELINE GEOMETRY GENERAL SHAPE OF THE SHORELINE AT THE POINT OF INTEREST PLUS 200 METERS (660 FT) ON EITHER SIDE	Score: 0 — COVE		Score: 2 — IRREGULAR SHORELINE		Score: 4 — HEADLAND OR STRAIGHT SHORELINE		
d. SHORE SLOPE SLOPE OF THE PLANTING AREA (VERTICAL TO HORIZONTAL)	Score: 0 — GRADUAL 1 to 15 OR LESS			Score: 4 — STEEP MORE THAN 1 to 15			
e. SEDIMENT GRAIN SIZE OF SEDIMENTS	Score: 0 — SILT & CLAY	Score: 2 — FINE SAND	Score: 4 — MEDIUM SAND	Score: 6 — COARSE SAND	Score: 8 — GRAVEL		
f. BOAT TRAFFIC PROXIMITY OF SITE TO NAVIGATION CHANNELS FOR LARGE VESSELS OR SMALL RECREATIONAL CRAFT	Score: 0 — NO NAVIGATION CHANNEL WITHIN 1 KILOMETER (0.6 MILES)		Score: 8 — NAVIGATION CHANNEL WITHIN 1 KILOMETER (0.6 MILES)		Score: 16 — NAVIGATION CHANNEL WITHIN 100 METERS (330 FT)		
g. WIND THE ORIENTATION OF THE SITE IN RELATION TO LOCAL WINDS	Score: 0 — SHELTERED FROM WIND		Score: 4 — DOES NOT FACE IN THE DIRECTION OF PREVAILING WINDS OR FREQUENT STORM WINDS		Score: 8 — FACES IN THE DIRECTION OF PREVAILING WINDS OR FREQUENT STORM WINDS		

4. CUMULATIVE WAVE CLIMATE SCORE ____

SCORE = 1 TO 10: USE SPRIGS AT 3-FOOT SPACINGS IN 10-FOOT (MINIMUM) ZONES.

= 11 TO 20: USE SPRIGS OR 15-WEEK SEEDLINGS AT 1½-FOOT SPACINGS IN 10-FOOT (MINIMUM) ZONES.

= 21 TO 30: USE 5-7 MONTH SEEDLINGS OR PLUGS AT 1½-FOOT SPACINGS IN 20-FOOT (MINIMUM) ZONES.

= ABOVE 30: DO NOT PLANT

Figure 87   Site Evaluation Form for Marsh Plants
[After U.S. Army Corps of Engineers (1980)]

Black Needle Rush *(juncus roemerianus)*. This species is extensive along the Atlantic coast south of New England. It is found in high marshes where it is flooded only by winddriven tides or in areas near the edge of uplands where freshwater seepage regularly occurs. It is a good stabilizer, although difficult to propagate, yet under favorable conditions it will invade areas already populated by cordgrasses.

Common Reed *(Phragmites communis)*. The common reed grows 4.5 to 12 feet tall and is widely distributed in brackish (salinity range 1 to 35 ppt) to freshwater areas above the mean high water level. It is easy to transplant and provides good stability; however, it does tend to compete with other plants and may become a nuisance by crowding out more desirable species.

Mangroves. Three species of mangrove--black *(Avicennia germinans)*, red *(Rhizophora mangle)*, and white *(Laguncularia racemosa)*--occur along the south Atlantic coast, primarily in Florida. Mangroves are good stabilizers, but they require considerably more time (2 or 3 years) than grasses to become established. During this time, the plants are susceptible to possible damage from tides, traffic, and browsing animals. Mangrove seeds, seedlings, or plants are best planted in established cordgrass stands, which provide stability until the mangroves are established.

Slow-release (e.g., osmocote) or a magnesium-ammonium phosphate fertilizer can be placed in the planting hole if needed, especially for the larger transplants. Daily watering may be required if flooding does not occur.

Gulf Coast Marshes. The vegetation found in gulf coast marshes does not substantially differ from south Atlantic coast marshes. Grasses, primarily saltgrass and gulf cordgrass, are prevalent, while smooth cordgrass, saltmeadow cordgrass, and black needle rush are also common.

Gulf Cordgrass *(Spartina spartinae)*. Gulf cordgrass is found along the gulf coast from southwest Louisiana to Texas. It performs well above the mean high water level. It is propagated like saltmeadow cordgrass, using the same procedure.

Saltgrass *(Distichlis spicata)* - Saltgrass is generally limited to the more saline, high marshes along the gulf coast. The plant is usually found in a mixture with saltmeadow cordgrass or black needle rush, and is rarely the dominant species except in poorly drained areas or in narrow bands. Saltgrass is more difficult to establish than the cordgrasses and usually is allowed to volunteer into cordgrass plantings.

Pacific Coast Marshes. Vegetation in marshes along the Pacific coast is more diverse than along the Atlantic coast.

Pacific cordgrass is found along the central and southern California coasts. Pickleweed, sedges, arrowgrass, and tufted hair grass are common along the northern Pacific coast.

Pacific Cordgrass *(Spartina foliosa)*. It is similar to smooth cordgrass, but it takes longer to establish. It dominates below the mean tide level of intertidal marshes. Plants and sprigs should be inserted by hand in holes made in soft, fine-textured soils. Fertilizers should contain equal quantities of available nitrogen and phosphate.

Pickleweed *(Salicornia spp.)*. From mean high water to extreme high tide, various species of pickleweed can be used upslope of Pacific cordgrass. It will spread both by seeds and vegetatively (by rhizomes and tillers), but because it is shallow-rooted, it is probably not as useful for stabilization as Pacific cordgrass. Pickleweed may be easily established by seeding or by transplanted peat-pot seedlings, and in fact, it often invades disturbed surfaces during the first growing season.

Sedge *(Carex lyngbvei)*. Sedge marshes are usually found in areas such as river deltas where silty soils exist. They grow above the mean tide level and are not especially salt tolerant. The plant may respond to nitrogen and phosphorous under deficient conditions. It appears to be one of the best marsh plants available in the Pacific Northwest.

Tufted Hair Grass *(Deschampsia caespitosa)*. This plant predominates i high marshes subject to flooding only by higher-high tides. It is a good sediment accumulator and stabilizer once established. It is generally easy to transplant and quick to establish.

Arrowgrass *(Triglochlin maritima)*. This plant will frequently invade and colonize disturbed marshes, trapping sediments and debris and helping to create a substrate for other plants. Planting should follow the method described for sedges.

Great Lakes Marshes. Marshes of the Great Lakes are generally limited in extent, and confined primarily to the protected shores of bays and inlets of Lakes Huron and Michigan. Establishing fresh water marshes may not provide as satisfactory a level of erosion prevention as saltwater marshes. The landowner interested in establishing fresh water marshes should consider the common reed *(Phragmites communis), rushes (Scirpus spp.)* such as spike rush, bulrush, and great bulrush, and, in some instances, upland grasses such as reed canarygrass *(Phalaris arundinacea)*.

Beach and Dune Plants

The protection of the upland portions of sandy shorelines can be accomplished through the creation of barrier dunes and the stabilization of present dunes. Vegetation used to initiate the building of barrier dunes is specially adapted to the more severe environment of the beach area (Figure 55). Barrier dune formation can occur naturally, but it is usually slow and in some areas does not happen. Utilization and proper management of the natural processes can accelerate the development.

Figure 88   Dune Vegetation

The beach provides a generally harsh environment for plant growth. Plants must tolerate rapid sand accumulation, flooding, salt spray, sandblasts, wind and water erosion, wide temperature fluctuations, drought, and low nutrient levels. Plants capable of stabilizing coastal dunes, however, occur in most coastal regions where there is sufficient rainfall to support plant growth. These regions and several of the most successful species are discussed below.

Planting specifications for several selected beach grass species are summarized in Table 19.

Table 19

SELECTED BEACH AND DUNE GRASS PLANTING SPECIFICATIONS

Element	Beach Grass American	Beach Grass Panic	Beach Grass European	Sea Oats*
Planting Season				
Late fall to early winter	Yes[+]	Yes	Yes	No
Midwinter	Yes[+]	Optimum	Yes	Optimum
Late winter to early spring	Optimum[+]	Optimum	Optimum	Yes
Early spring to mid-spring	Yes	Yes	Yes	No
Available Source				
Transplants				
Commercial	Yes	Yes	Yes	Yes
Wild harvest	Yes	Yes	Yes	Yes
Seed				
Commercial	No	No	No	No
Wild harvest	Yes	Yes	Yes	Yes
Planting Density				
Eroding site	18-inch centers	18-inch centers	18-inch centers	18-inch centers
Noneroding site	24-inch centers	24-inch centers	24-inch centers	24-inch centers
Stems per transplant	3	1	3	1
Fertilization, First Growing Season				
Composition NPK[a]	3-1-0[o]	2-1-1	7-0-0	2-1-1
Rate lbs/acre (annual)	200	24	40	240
Application periods	March	April	April	April
(equal applications in	May	June		June
months indicated)	July	August		August
	September			

* Illegal to harvest in some states.

[+] Season not recommended for Great Lakes.

[a] NPK--Nitrogen-Phosphorous-Potassium.

[o] 3-1-1 in Great Lakes.

[After U.S. Army Corps of Engineers (1977c)]

North Atlantic Region. Extending from the Canadian border to the Virginia capes, American beachgrass is the dominant dune stabilizing plant in this region; bitter panicum offers promise as a companion plant.

American Beachgrass (Ammophila breviligulata). This species is probably the most widely used for the initial stabilization of blowing sand because it grows rapidly and can effectively trap sand by the middle of the first growing season. Once established, it multiplies quickly. It prefers cool weather and plants start growing in early spring and continue through fall under the most favorable conditions. The grass can be transplanted over a long planting season with a good chance of survival. American beachgrass is available commercially or may also be harvested from wild stands. Seedlings are the preferred method of planting. Starting from seed is usually uneconomical because seed supplies are unreliable and weeds are difficult to control.

Bitter Panicum (Panicum amarum). This grass is indigenous along the Atlantic coast from Connecticut southward. It is best used as a companion to American beachgrass, especially in those areas where the beachgrass is subject to severe attack by the disease, soft scale.

South Atlantic Region. This region extends from the Virginia capes to Key West. Sea oats is the dominant plant; however, both American beachgrass and bitter panicum will successfully establish dunes, when planted in combination with sea oats, especially in the northern part of the region.

Sea Oats *(Uniola paniculata)*. More persistent than other stabilizing species, sea oats does not provide much initial protection. It grows slowly, is difficult to propagate, and is not widely available commercially. However, once established, sea oats provide excellent protection. To provide initial protection, sea oats should be planted in mixes with American beachgrass and bitter panicum to the Carolinas and with bitter panicum farther south. As the other grasses thin out, sea oats will spread and dominate the dune.

Saltmeadow Cordgrass *(Spartina patens)*. This plant is more commonly used in marsh plantings (see prior discussion), but it will frequently invade a beach area and create small dunes, which will support other vegetation. It is particularly well suited for this use on low, moist sites where periodic salt buildup occurs.

Bermuda Grass *(Cynodon dactglon)*. Although this is not a prominent dune species, it can be used very effectively in special situations. The coastal hybrid is deep rooting and rapidly establishing and can be used to revegetate areas where American beachgrass   has been killed by insects or disease. Turf hybrids will, when properly managed, perform well on the dune environment, where they form a more traffic resistant stand than other types of vegetation.

Gulf Region. The region extends from the gulf coast of Florida to the Mexican border. Sea oats and bitter panicum are the dominant dune stabilizing species. Other species include railroad vine and saltmeadow cordgrass.   Establishment of sea oats, bitter panicum, and saltmeadow cordgrass should follow prior recommendations. Local variations exist, and the landowner should consult local agricultural extension agents and others about differences in technique and management of plantings of these species.

Railroad Vine. *(Ipomea pes-caprae)*. This plant is one of the more prominent pioneer species in this region. It is not generally planted because it is somewhat less effective in trapping sand than dune grasses. It is, however, capable of rapidly spreading over foredunes, and transplants of the vine may be included as part of a grass establishment planting.

North Pacific Region. This region extends from the Canadian border to Monterey, California. European beachgrass and American dunegrass are the dominant sand stabilizing plants of the region. American beachgrass may also be applicable in the area.

European Beachgrass *(Ammophila arenaria)*. This plant is inexpensive and used widely in this region. Although it effectively traps sand, it forms dense stands with little outward spread, causing the resulting dunes to have steep windward slopes. Another disadvantage is that it will often exclude native species, making it difficult to establish mixed plantings.

American Dunegrass *(Elymus mollis)*. Although this grass is native to the northwest, it is more difficult and expensive to propagate than either European or American beachgrass. The grass tends to produce low, gently sloping dunes, often preferable to those dunes built by European beachgrass.

American dunegrass should be set 12 inches or more deep in moist sand. Satisfactory planting occurs primarily in the months when the grass is dormant; late November through February in the northern portion of the region, and not at all in the southern extent. Planting should be limited to temperatures below 55 degrees F. Planting several stems per hill would be desired; however, due to the expense, a close spacing of 12 inches with one viable stem makes better use of scarce planting stock. An application of 35 pounds of nitrogen per acre from a soluble source is recommended to maintain the plants once established.

South Pacific Region. This region extends from Monterey, California, to the Mexican border. While some of the beach grasses discussed above (e.g. , European beachgrass) are applicable in the northern portions of this region, the dominant plants are forbs such as the Sea Fig *(Carpobrotus edulis and C. aequilaterus)*. These are effective for sand stabilization but are not good dune builders.

Great Lakes Region. Dune development is mostly confined to the Michigan and Indiana shores of Lake Michigan; however, the discussion, which follows, is applicable to all the shores of the Great Lakes. American beachgrass is the dominant species. Native species, especially prairie sandreed, will often invade naturally. Once the dunes have been stabilized, volunteer or planted species of upland vegetation can be established. Species of grasses suggested would include reed canarygrass, big bluestem, little bluestem, and switchgrass, all native to the area. These grasses may be planted from early May to the middle of June at a rate of about 0.5 pounds of seed per 1000 square feet. All require full sun and may be mowed occasionally. Reed canarygrass is especially useful in wet spots.

Various ground covers may also be planted. The species which may be utilized are best suggested by local agricultural experts. The same holds true for shrubs and trees.

An additional problem, which landowners in the Great Lakes region have, is the stabilization of bluffs. Often, structural corrections are required in concert with vegetation. Once the structural stabilization is accomplished, vegetative cover will aid in preventing erosion, reducing seepage, and slowing runoff.

The type of vegetation, which can be established on bluff slopes, is dependent upon the slope angle. Slopes steeper than 1 on 1 generally preclude successful vegetation; slopes flatter than 1 on 3 can be planted as a lawn and maintained in the usual manner. Slopes between 1 on 3 and 1 on 1 can be planted with grasses which will not be mowed, ground covers, trees and shrubs, or combinations of these three. As mentioned before, local expertise (e.g., agricultural extension agents) can aid the landowner in selecting suitable species, and in describing the most practical methods of establishment and maintenance.

PERCHED BEACHES

Perched beaches are constructed by placing sand fill behind a low breakwater or sill. Sills can be constructed of virtually any material described earlier for fixed breakwaters. Beach material should be chosen in accordance with guidelines previously given for beach fills. Proper filtering should be provided beneath and behind the sill to prevent settlement and loss of retained fill. In some cases, navigation markers may be required.

Sheet Piling. Sheet pile sills are similar to bulkheads. Timber sheet piling will generally require filter cloth backing on the shoreward face to prevent loss of the retained sand backfill through joints in the structure. This is not generally a problem with steel or aluminum sheet piling. Sheet pile sills also form an abrupt step to deeper water, which would definitely be hazardous to bathers, particularly children.

The same precautions regarding adequate ground penetration and toe protection for a bulkhead also apply to a sheet pile sill.

Concrete Boxes. Precast, open concrete boxes (for use in drainage structures) can be placed side by side and filled with sand to form a sill (Figure 57). During placement, the gaps between adjacent boxes must be minimized to prevent excessive wave transmission through the structure and to help retain the perched beach. Filter cloth backing is required and toe protection
should be provided on the offshore side.

Figure 89   Concrete Box Sill

PROPRIETARY DEVICES AND SPECIALTY MATERIALS

The devices and many materials in this report are not generally available or familiar to local suppliers. Table 7 covers principal manufacturers that are active nationwide. Inclusion of manufacturers in this directory does not necessarily represent endorsement or recommendation by the government. In fact, some items listed herein were not recommended for specific applications in this guidebook. (WARNING! The accuracy of the following information has not been verified since the original publication of this document.)

Table 20

Device or Material	Manufacturer

DuPont Company
Room 38095
Wilmington, Delaware 19898
(Nonwoven)

Menardi-Southern
Division of United States Filter
Soil and Erosion Control Department
Headquarters
3908 Colgate
Houston, Texas 77017
713/643-6513
(Woven and Nonwoven)

Nicolon Corporation
Erosion Control Products
Suite 1990
Peachtree Corners Plaza
Norcross (Atlanta), Georgia 30071
404/447-6272
800/241-9691
(Woven)

Erosion Control Products, Inc.
Route 5
Box 406
Daphne, Alabama 36526
205/626-3510
(Woven and Nonwoven)

Device or Material	Manufacturer
Gabions	Terra Aqua Corporation Division of Bekaert Steel Wire Corporation P. O. Box 7546 Reno, Nevada 89510 702/329-6262
	Maccaferri Gabions, Inc. P.O. Box 43A Williamsport, MD 21795 301/223-8700
Gobi Blocks Gobimat	Nicolon Corporation Erosion Control Products Suite 1990 Peachtree Corners Plaza Norcross (Atlanta), Georgia 30071 404/447-6272 800/241-9691
Jumbo Blocks Jumbo Ercomats	Erosion Control Systems, Inc. 3349 Ridgelake Drive Suite 101-B Metairie, Louisiana 70002 504/834-5650
Lok-Gard Blocks	Coastal Research Corporation 1100 Crain Highway, S.W. Glen Burnie, Maryland 21061 301/761-0584
Longard Tube	Edward E. Gillen Company 218 West Becher Street Milwaukee, Wisconsin 53207 414/744-9824
Nami Ring	Robert Q. Palmer 5027 Justin Drive, N.W. Alburquerque, New Mexico 87114
Sandgrabber	Sandgrabber, Inc. 3105 Old Kawkawlin Road Bay City, Michigan 48706 517/686-6601

Device or Material	Manufacturer
Surgebreaker	Great Lakes Environmental Marine, Ltd. 39 South LaSalle Street Chicago, Illinois 60603 312/332-3377
Terrafix Blocks	Erosion Control Products, Inc. 9151 Fairgrounds Road West Palm Beach, Florida 33411 305/793-5650
Turfblock (Monoslab)	Anchor Block Company P. 0. Box 3360 St. Paul, Minnesota 55165 612/777-8321
Wave-Maze	Robert L. Stitt 10732 E. Freer Street Temple City, California
Z-Wall	The Fanwall Corporation 670 Old Connecticut Road Farmingham, Massachusetts 01701 617/879-3350

OVERVIEW OF THE DESIGN PROBLEM

CHARACTERIZATION OF THE SITE

The site to be considered is a sheltered location within an estuary. The shoreline is a low bluff about 9 feet high. At mean low water (MLW), it is fronted by a 15 ft. wide beach. The Stillwater level is at the toe of the bluff at mean high water (MHW). The bluff slope is approximately 1:1, and the soil is fine-grained, mostly sand and silt, with a heavy overgrowth of brush and other plants. The number of trees standing in the water and lying on the beach is evidence of a long-term and chronic erosion problem. The beach itself consists of fine to coarse grained material, mostly sand, but with s significant fraction of gravel and cobbles. The offshore bottom slope is approximately 1 on 33.

Figure 90   Design Problem Site

WATER LEVELS

The spring tide range and the mean tide level were determined by reference to Tide Tables [US Department of Commerce (1976)]. Local experience indicated that 2 feet of storm setup was appropriate. The site profile and water levels are summarized on Figure 91.

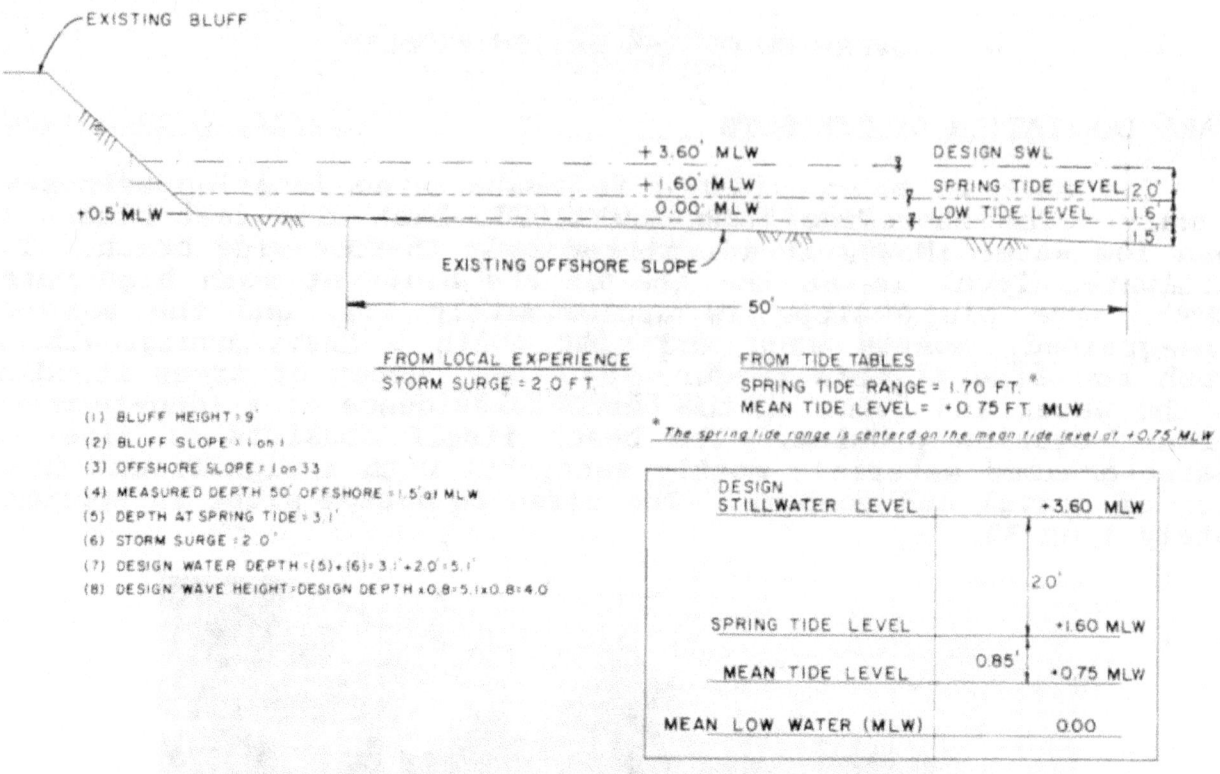

Figure 91   Profile and Physical Conditions at the Site

WAVE CONDITIONS

The fastest-mile wind speed for the site is:

    10-year: 65 mph

Fetch lengths at the site were displayed earlier on Figure 17. This is reproduced as figure 92 for the convenience of the reader.

Fetch Line 1
        Length: 2.80 nm x 1.15 = 3.22 mi
             2.80 nm x 6080 = 17, 025 ft

        Average Depth: 7.2 ft at MLW
                10.8 ft at design Stillwater level

Fetch Line 2
        Length: 2.10 nm x 1.15 = 2.41 mi
             2.10 nm x 6080 = 12,770 ft

        Average Depth: 11.6 ft at MLW
                15.2 ft at design Stillwater level

Using tables 5 to 9, or equations 5 and 6, find the design wave height and period (10 year return period).

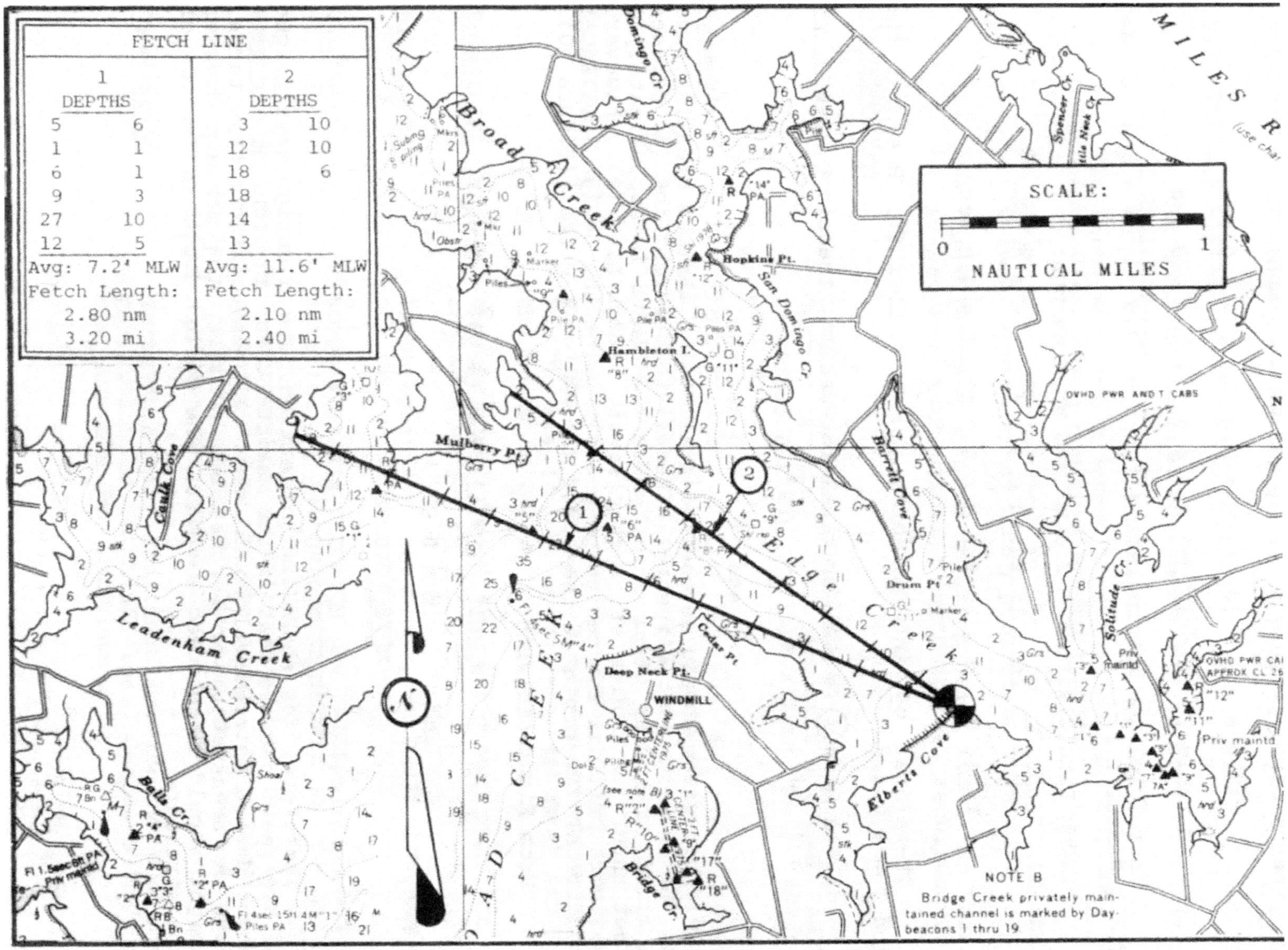

Figure 92   Fetch Lengths at the Site

Fetch Line 1 with F = 3.2 mi and WS = 65 mph:

> Table 6: d = 10 ft; H = 3.0 ft; T= 4.0 sec
> Table 7: d = 15 ft; H = 4.0 ft; T= 4.0 sec

Fetch Line 2 with F= 2.4 mi and WS = 65 mph:

> Table 6: d = 15 ft; H = 3.5 ft; T= 4.0 sec
> Table 7: d = 20 ft; H = 4.0 ft; T= 4.0 sec

Therefore, by interpolating for d = 10.8 ft; H = 3.2 ft; amd T = 4.0 sec.

Fetch line 2 is more critical for design. Therefore, use H= 3.5 ft and T = 4.0 sec.

This value should be checked against the maximum breaking wave at the site or just offshore. (Recall that Fetch Line 1 crosses a shoal area near cedar point where the depth is approximately 3 feet under the design Stillwater level. Fetch Line 2, however, was more critical for design purposes). With the design Stillwater condition, the depth at the bluff toe, d_s = 3.2 feet (Figure 90).

From Figure 18 with,

$$D_s/gT^2 = (3.1)/32.2 \ (4.0)^2 = 0.0060,$$

and m = 0.03, H_b/d_s = 0.98

Therefore, H_b = 3.1 x 0.98 = 3.0 ft.

Therefore, for shoreline protection, use a design wave height of 3.0 ft, because that is the maximum that can occur at the site under design water level conditions. For any offshore structures, such as breakwaters or perched beach sills, the maximum breaker height should be checked based on design depth at the toe of the structure.

SELECTION OF DEVICES

Landowner's Criteria

No Action	Inappropriate. Unacceptable to the landowner. Current erosion rates represent a considerable financial loss at prevailing real estate prices.
Relocate	Inappropriate. The land is now undeveloped. The owner will build a retirement home with large setback from the shore. He desires to stop erosion now.
Bulkhead	Appropriate. Equipment access to the job sit presents no problems. Steps can be added late for access to the dock. Recreational use of the beach is not a high priority.
Revetment	Appropriate. There is sufficient room for a regarded slope.
Breakwaters	Inappropriate. Scour at the bluff toe would not be positively prevented.
Groins	Inappropriate. There is little sand-sized material in alongshore transport at the site.
Beach Fill	Inappropriate. Fill provides no positive protection against toe scour. No recreation beach is desired. The plan must have minim maintenance requirements.
Vegetation	Inappropriate. Plantings provide no positive protection to the bluff toe. Coarse soils are not suitable for plantings.
Infiltration and Drainage Controls	Inappropriate. Drainage and infiltration are not problems at this site.
Slope Flattening	Inappropriate. Suitable only in combination with a revetment. Slope stability is not a basic problem.

PERMIT REQUIREMENTS

Federal, state, and possibly local permits are required for construction in, across, under, or on the banks of navigable waters of the United States. Federal permits are coordinated by the applicant and the states through division and district offices of the U. S. Army Corps of Engineers. The authority for the Corps' permit program is derived basically from two laws: Section 10 of the River and Harbor Act of 1899 and Section 404 of the Clean Water Act of 1977, as amended. Section 10 of the 1899 Act requires permits for structures and dredging in navigable waters of the United States, which are those coastal waters subject to tidal action shoreward of the mean high water line, and inland waters that have been used, are now used, or may be used in the future for interstate or foreign commerce. In tidal areas, this includes all land below the mean high water line.

On the Great Lakes, permits are required under this section for construction lakeward of the highwater mark, the definition of which varies from state to state, and often with the federal definition. Where doubt exists, an appropriate local state agency or Corps district office can provide assistance.

Section 404 of the Clean Water Act mandates a Corps permit for placement of dredged or fill material in waters of the United States, which includes navigable waters as under Section 10 permits, as well as tributaries and wetlands adjacent to navigable waters of the United States. Jurisdiction extends inland to the headwaters of streams at a point where the average flow is five cubic feet per second. Wetlands are defined as "those areas that are inundated or saturated by surface or ground water at a frequency and duration sufficient to support, and than under normal conditions do support, a prevalence of vegetation typically adapted for life in saturated soil conditions. Wetlands generally include swamps, marshes, bogs and similar areas" [U.S. Army, Corps of Engineers (1977b)].

A standard application form (ENG Form 4345) must be obtained from the local Corps district office. The application must include a description of the proposed construction, including "necessary drawings, sketches, or plans; the location, purpose, and intended use of the proposed activity; scheduling of the activity; the names and addresses of adjoining property owners; the location and dimensions of adjacent structures; and the approvals required by other federal, interstate, state or local agencies for the work, including all approvals received or denials already made" [U.S. Army, Corps of Engineers (1977b)].

Upon the receipt of the application, a public notice inviting comments on the application is normally issued. The comment period is generally 30 days, although it may be longer or shorter depending on the circumstances. Applications are generally coordinated with the appropriate federal, state, and local agencies as well as adjoining property owners sometimes leading to comments that require modification of the original proposal. Beyond these possible modifications, if the comments received and the study conducted by the Corps reveal no overriding public interest or environmental problems, the application would then be approved and a permit issued. Although variations exist, the process normally requires 75 to 90 days for routine applications Controversial applications can take considerably longer.

The Corps has adopted a number of conditional general permits on a regional and nationwide basis to reduce red tape and paperwork. No separate application is required for activities where general permits have been issued. Applicants should check with the local District Engineer to determine if the proposed work is covered by a general permit and what conditions may apply.

Additional information pertinent to local areas is available -through Corps of Engineers' district offices or certain state and local agencies. Permit applications should be initialed early to avoid unnecessary delays later.

OTHER HELP

CORPS OF ENGINEERS OFFICES

Permits are coordinated through district of f ices of the Corps of Engineers. Corps offices are also possible sources of information on water levels, wave climate, and other physical site conditions. Mail addresses, office locations, and phone numbers for Corps personnel familiar with coastal processes are given in Table 21. (**WARNING!** The following information has not been verified since the original publication of this document)

Table 21
CORPS OF ENGINEERS OFFICES

Address	Phone	Jurisdiction
U. S. Army Engineering Division, New England 424 Trapelo Road Waltham, Massachusetts 02154	617/894-2400 X-554	Atlantic coast from Maine to the Connecticut-New York Line
U. S. Army Engineering District, New York 26 Federal Plaza New York, New York 10007	212/264-5174	Atlantic coast of New York and the New Jersey coast north of Manasquan Inlet
U. S. Army Engineering District, Philadelphia U. S. Custon House 2nd and Chestnut Street Philadelphia, Pennsylvania 19106	215/597-4714	Atlantic coast of New Jersey and Delaware from Manasquan Inlet, south to the Delaware-Maryland Line, including Delaware Bay and the C&D Canal
U. S. Army Engineering District, Baltimore P. 0. Box 1715 Baltimore, Maryland 21203 Office Location: 31 Hopkins Plaza Baltimore, Maryland 21201	301/962-2545	Atlantic and Chesapeake Bay shorelines of Maryland
U. S. Army Engineering District, Norfolk 803 Front Street Norfolk, Virginia 23510	804/441-3764	Atlantic and Chesapeake Bay shorelines of Virginia
U. S. Army Engineering District, Wilmington P. 0. Box 1980 Wilmington, North Carolina 28402 Office Location: 308 Federal Building Wilmington, North Carolina	919/343-4778	Atlantic coast and interior bays and sounds of North Carolina
U. S. Army Engineering District, Charleston P. 0. Box 919 Charleston, South Carolina 29402 Office Location: Federal Building 334 Meeting Street Charleston, South Carolina 29402	803/724-4248	Atlantic Coast of South Carolina

Address	Phone	Jurisdiction
U. S Army Engineering District, Savannah P. 0. Box 889 Savannah, Georgia 31402 Office Location: 200 E Saint Julian Street Savannah, Georgia 31402	912/944-5502	Atlantic coast of Georgia
U. S. Army Engineer District, Jacksonville P. 0. Box 4970 Jacksonville, Florida 32201 Office Location: 400 West Bay Street Jacksonville, Florida 32202	904/791-2204	Atlantic coast of Florida and Gulf coast of Florida to the St. Marks River
U. S. Army Engineering District, Mobile P. 0. Box 2288 Mobile, Alabama 36628 Office Location: 109 St. Joseph Street Mobile, Alabama 36602	205/690-3482	Gulf Coast of Florida from the St. Marks River west Louisiana-Mississippi line
U. S. Army Engineering District, New Orleans P. 0. Box 60267 New Orleans, Louisiana 70160 Office Location: Foot of Prytania Street New Orleans, Louisiana 70160	504/838-2480	Gulf coast of Louisiana
U.S. Army Engineering District, Galveston P.0. Box 1229 Galveston, Texas 77553 Office Location: 110 Essayons Boulevard 400 Barracuda Avenue Galveston, Texas 77550	713/764-1211 X -314	Gulf coast of Texas
U.S. Army Engineering District, Los Angeles P.0. Box 2711 Los Angeles, California 90053 Office Location: 300 North Los Angeles Street Los Angeles, California 90012	213/688-6400	Pacific coast of CA from the Mexican border North to Cape San Martin
U. S. Army Engineering District, San Francisco 211 Main Street San Francisco, California 94105	415/556-5370	Pacific coast of CA from Cape San Martin north to the CA-OR line including San Francisco Bay
U.S. Army Engineering District, Portland P.0. Box 2946 Portland, Oregon 97208 Office Location: Mulnomah Building 319 S.W. Pine Portland, Oregon 97204	503/221-6477	Pacific coast of Oregon

Address	Phone	Jurisdiction
U.S. Army Engineering District, Seattle P.O. Box C-3755 Seattle, Washington 98124 Office Location: 4735 East Marginal Way South Seattle, Washington	206/764-3555	Pacific coast of Washington and Puget Sound
U.S. Army Engineering District, Alaska P.O. Box 7002 Anchorage, Alaska 99510 Office Location: Building 21-700 Elmendorf Air Force Base, Alaska	907/752-3925	Coast of Alaska
U. S. Army Engineering Division, Pacific Ocean Building 230 Ft. Shafter, Hawaii 96858	808/438-2837	Hawaii and the Pacific Trust Territories
U.S. Army Engineering District, Detroit P.O. Box 1027 Detroit, Michigan 48231 Office Location: Patrick V. McNamara Building R 477 Michigan Avenue Detroit, Michigan 48226	313/226-6791	U.S. shorelines of Lakes Superior, Huron and St. Clair; the Lake Michigan Shoreline except in IL and IN, Lake Erie shoreline of MI
U. S. Army Engineering District, Chicago 219 S. Dearborn Street Chicago, Illinois 60604	312/353-0789	Lake Michigan shoreline of IL and IN
U. S. Army Engineering District, Buffalo 1776 Niagara Street Buffalo, New York 14207	716/876-5454 x-2230	U.S. shorelines of Lake Ontario and Erie except in Michigan

Table 22

State   Office Address and Phone Number

<u>State</u>   <u>Office Address and Phone Number</u>

State   Office Address and Phone Number

Hydrographic Charts

Hydrographic charts are available for a small fee for all U.S. coastal waters. These provide information on water depths and fetch lengths to determine exposure of a site to wave action. Identification of a specific chart and important information about the available chart series are in the following Nautical Catalogs. (**WARNING!** The accuracy of the following information has not been verified since the original publication of this document.)

Catalog No. 1 - Atlantic and Gulf Coasts
Catalog No. 2 - Pacific Coast and Hawaii
Catalog No. 3 - Alaska
Catalog No. 4 - Great Lakes

For information or mail orders write to:

Distribution Division, C44
National Ocean Survey
Riverdale, Maryland 20840
301/436-6990

Counter sales are also available at that location as well as regional offices of the National Ocean Survey at:

439 West York Street
Norfolk, Virginia 23510 and

1801 Fairview Avenue East
Seattle, Washington 90102

Charts can also be obtained from the U. S. Coast Guard at the locations below.

3rd District
Governors Island
New York, New York 10004

9th District
1240 East 9th Street
Cleveland, Ohio 44199

Water Levels

Tide Tables are available for all coastal areas of the United States. These contain predictions of high and low tide elevations and their time of occurrence for one calendar year at primary tide stations. Values of time and elevation differences from the primary station are also given for numerous secondary stations, as are normal and spring tide ranges for all stations. Tide Tables are available from the Distribution Division, National Ocean Survey, at the address above.

Lake levels are also available in summary form through the Monthly Bulletin of Lake Levels for the Great Lakes. This contains the current level for each lake, a six-month projection of future lake levels, and historic high and low lake levels. The Monthly Bulletin is available, free, from the:

Department of the Army
Detroit District, Corps of Engineers
P. 0. Box 1027
Detroit, Michigan 48231

SUGGESTED READING

Numerous booklets, brochures, and reports, many of them free, are available for further study in selected topics and subjects presented in this report. Most government reports include either their NTIS or GPO accession numbers. Use the NTIS number to order documents from:

National Technical Information Service (NTIS)
5285 Port Royal Road
Springfield, VA 22161
(703) 605-6000
http://www.ntis.gov/

Use the GPO number to order documents from:

Superintendent of Documents
US Government Printing Office (GPO)
PO Box 371954
Pittsburg, PA 15250-7954
(866) 512-1800 (toll free)
http://www.gpo.gov

Shore and Lake Processes

Beach Processes and Sedimentation, Komar, P., Prentice-Hall, Englewood Cliffs, New Jersey, 1976, 464 pp.

Coastal Processes and Beach Erosion, Caldwell, J. M., Reprint 1-67, U. S. Army Coastal Engineering Research Center, January 1967, (NTIS #652 025).

Ebb and Flow: The Tides of Earth, Air and Water, Defant, A., Ann Arbor Science Library Series, University of Michigan Press, Ann Arbor, Michigan, 1958.

Land Against the Sea, Rayner, A. C., editor, Miscellaneous Paper 4-64, U. S. Army Coastal Engineering Research Center, May 1964, (NTIS #453 227).

Our New Beach: How It Works, Dade County Beach Erosion Control and Hurricane Protection Project, U. S. Army Engineer District, Jacksonville, Jacksonville, Florida, 20 pp., (free).

A Primer of Basic Concepts of Lakeshore Processes, Duane, D. B., et. al., Miscellaneous Paper 1-75, U. S. Army Coastal Engineering Research Center, January 1975, (NTIS# A008 010).

Waves and Beaches: The Dynamics of the Ocean Surface, Bascom, W., Anchor Books, Garden City, New York, 1964.

Shore Protection (General)

Consumer Investment in Shoreline Protection, Braden, P., Michigan Sea Grant Program, 2200 Bonisteel Boulevard, Ann Arbor, Michigan 48109.

Harmony With the Lake: Guide *to Bluff Stabilization,* Division of Water Resources, Illinois Department of Transportation, Room 1010, Marina City Office Building, 300 North State Street, Chicago, Illinois 60610, (free).

Help Yourself, North Central Division, U. S. Army Corps of Engineers, 536 South Clark Street, Chicago, Illinois 60605, (free).

Low Cost Shore Protection: Final Report on the Shoreline Erosion Control Demonstration Program, Office, Chief of Engineers, U. S. Army Corps of Engineers, Washington, D. C., (1981).

The Michigan Demonstration Erosion Control Program in 1976, Brater, E. F., et al., University of Michigan Coastal Zone Laboratory, Michigan Sea Grant Technical Report No. 55, February 1977.

Shore and Beach, American Shore and Beach Preservation Association, P. 0. Drawer 2087, Wilmington, North Carolina 28401, (published quarterly; $20 annually).

Shore Erosion Control: A Guide *for Waterfront Property Owners in the Chesapeake Bag Area,* Baltimore District, U. S. Army Corps of Engineers, P. 0. Box 1715, Baltimore, Maryland 21203, 62 pp., (free).

Shoreline Erosion Control, Philadelphia District, U. S. Army Corps of Engineers, Attention: NAPEN-P (SECDP), Custom House, Second and Chestnut Street, Philadelphia, Pennsylvania 19106, (free).

Shore Protection Guidelines: National Shoreline Study, office, Chief of Engineers, U. S. Army Corps of Engineers, Washington, D.C., August 1971, 59 pp.
Shore Protection Manual (Vols. I, II, and III), U. S. Army Corps of Engineers, Coastal Engineering Research Center, 1977, (GPO Stock No. 008-022-00113-1).

Waves Against the Shore: An Erosion Manual for the Great Lakes Region, Lake Michigan Federation, 53 West Jackson Boulevard, Suite 1710, Chicago, Illinois 60604, January 1978.

What You May Need to Know About Owning Shore Property, Great Lakes Communicator, Volume II, No. 5, February 1981.

Shore Protection Design

AWPI Technical Guidelines for Pressure-Treated Wood (1970).
S2 Bulkheads: Design and Construction - Part I
S3 Bulkheads: Design and Construction - Part II
S4 Bulkheads: Design and Construction - Part III
S5 Bulkheads: Hardware and Fasteners
Pl Timber Piling

American Wood Preservers Institute, 1651 Old Meadow Road, McLean, Virginia 22101.

Building Salt Marshes Along the Coast of the Continental United States, Woodhouse, W. W., Special Report 4, U. S. Army Coastal Engineering Research Center, May 1979, (GPO #088-022-00133-6).

Concrete Shore Protection, Portland Cement Association, 33 West Grand Avenue, Chicago, Illinois, 1955.

Designing for Bank Erosion Control with Vegetation, Knuston, P. L., Reprint 78-2, U. S. Army Coastal Engineering Research Center, February 1978, (NTIS #AO51 571).

*Designing Retaining Walls, Bulkheads and Seawalls of Treated Tim*ber, American Wood Preservers Institute, (address given above).

Factors Affecting the Durability of Concrete in Coastal Structures, Mather, B., Technical Memorandum 96, U. S. Army Beach Erosion Board, June 1957, (NTIS #158 634).

How to Build a Floating Scrap Tire Breakwater, Kowalski, T., Ross, **N.,** Marine Advisory Service, University of Rhode Island, Narragansett Bay Campus, Narragansett, Rhode Island 02882.

Planning Guidelines for Residential and Path Development in Michigan's Sand Dunes and Wetlands, Michigan Coastal Zone Management Program, Water Development Services Division, Michigan Department of Natural Resources, Lansing, Michigan.

Planting Guidelines for Marsh Development and Bank Stabilization, Knuston, P. L., Coastal Engineering Technical Aid 77-3, U. S. Army Coastal Engineering Research Center, August 1977, (NTIS #AO46 547).

The Role of Vegetation in Shoreline Management, Great Lakes Basin Commission, P. 0. Box 999, Ann Arbor, Michigan 48106, (single copies, free).

Permits and Regulations

Permit Program: A- Guide for Applicants, EP 1145-2-1, U. S. Army Corps of Engineers, Washington, D. C.

Regulations to Reduce Coastal Erosion, Wisconsin Coastal Zone Management Program, State Office of Planning and Energy, GEF II, 101 South Webster Street, Madison, Wisconsin 53702, (free).

GLOSSARY

Accretion - Accumulation of sand or other beach material at a point due to natural action of waves, currents and wind. A build-up of the beach.

Alongshore - Parallel to and near the shoreline; same as LONGSHORE.

Backhoe - Excavator similar to a power shovel except that the bucket faces the operator and is pulled toward him.

Bar - Fully or partly submerged mound of sand, gravel, or other unconsolidated material built on the bottom in shallow water by waves and currents.

Beach - Zone of sand or gravel extending from the low water line to a point landward where either the topography abruptly changes or permanent vegetation first appears.

Beach Fill - Sand or gravel placed on a beach by mechanical methods.

Beach, Perched - See PERCHED BEACH.

Bluff - High, steep bank at the water's edge. In common usage, a bank composed primarily of soil. See CLIFF.

Boulders - Large stones with diameters over 10 inches. Larger than COBBLES.

Breaker - A wave as it spills, plunges or collapses on a shore, natural obstruction, or man-made structure.

Breaker Zone - Area offshore where waves break.

Breaking Depth - Stillwater depth where waves break.

Breakwater - Structure aligned parallel to shore, sometimes shore connected, that provides protection from waves.

Bulkhead - A structure that retains or prevents sliding of land or protects the land from wave damage.

Clay - Extremely fine-grained soil with individual particles less than 0.00015 inches in diameter.

Cliff - High steep bank at the water's edge. In common usage, a bank composed primarily of rock. See BLUFF.

Cobbles - Rounded stones with diameters ranging from 3 to 10 inches. Cobbles are intermediate between GRAVEL and BOULDERS.

Crest - Upper edge or limit of a shore protection structure.

Cross Section - View of a structure or beach as if it were sliced by a vertical plane. The cross section should display structure, ground surface, and underlying material.

Culm - Single stem of grass.

Current - Flow of water in a given direction.

Current, Longshore - Current in the breaker zone moving essentially parallel to shore and usually caused by waves breaking at an angle to shore. Also called alongshore current.

Deep Water - Area where surf ace waves are not influenced by the bottom. Generally, a point where the depth is greater than one-half the surface wavelength.

Diffraction- Progressive reduction in wave height when a wave spreads into the shadow zone behind a barrier after the wave has passed its end.

Diurnal - Period or cycle lasting approximately one day. A diurnal tide has one high and one low in each cycle.

Downdrift - Direction of alongshore movement of littoral materials.

Dune - Hill, bank, bluff, ridge, or mound of loose, wind-blown material, usually sand.

Duration - Length of time the wind blows in nearly the same direction across a FETCH (generating area).

Ebb Tide - Part of the tidal cycle between high water and the next low. The falling tide.

Equilibrium - State of balance or equality of opposing forces.

Erosion - Wearing away of land by action of natural forces.

Fetch - Area where waves are generated by wind, which has steady direction and speed. Sometimes called FETCH LENGTH.

Fetch Length - Horizontal direction (in the wind direction) over which a wind generates waves. In sheltered waters, often the maximum distance that wind can blow across water.

Filter Cloth - Synthetic textile with openings for water to escape, but which prevents passage of soil particles.

Flood Tide - Part of the tidal cycle between low water and the next high. The rising tide.

Glacial Till - Unstratified glacial drift consisting of unsorted clay, sand, gravel, and boulders, intermingled.

Longshore - Parallel to and near the shoreline: same as ALONGSHORE.

Longshore Transport Rate - Rate of transport of littoral material parallel to shore. Usually expressed in cubic yards per year.

Low Tide - Minimum elevation reached by each falling tide.

Low Water Datum (LWD) - The elevation of each of the Great Lakes to which are referenced the depths shown on navigation charts and the authorized depths of navigation projects.

Marsh - Area of soft, wet, or periodically inundated land, generally treeless, and usually characterized by grasses and other low growth.

Mean Higher High Water (MHHW) - Average height of the daily higher high waters over a 19-year period. Only the higher high water of each pair of high waters of a tidal day is included in the mean.

Mean High Water (MHW) - Average height of the daily high waters over a 19-year period. For semidiurnal or mixed tides, the two high waters of each tidal day are included in the mean. For diurnal tides, the single daily high water is used to compute the mean.

Mean Lower Low Water (MLLW) - Average height of the daily lower-low waters of a 19-year period. Only the lower low water of each pair of low waters of a tidal day is included in the mean. Long used as the datum for Pacific coast navigation charts, it is now gradually being adopted for use across the United States.

Mean Low Water (MLW) - Average height of the low waters over a 19-year period. For semidiurnal and mixed tides, the two low waters of each   tidal day are included in the mean. For a diurnal tide, the one low water of each tidal day is used in the mean. Mean Low Water has been used as datum for many navigation charts published by the National Ocean Survey, but it is being phased out in favor of Mean Lower Low Water for all areas of the United States.

Mean Sea Level - Average height of the sea surface over a 19-year period. Not necessarily equal to MEAN TIDE LEVEL.

Mean Tide Level - Plane midway between MEAN HIGH WATER and MEAN LOW WATER. Not necessarily equal to MEAN SEA LEVEL. Also called half-tide level.

Mixed Tide - A tide in which there is a distinct difference in height between successive high and successive low waters. For mixed tides there are generally two high and two low waters each tidal day. Mixed tides may be described as intermediate between semidiurnal and diurnal tides.

Module - A structural component, a number of which are joined to make a whole.

Neap Tides - Tides with decreased ranges that occur when the moon is at first or last-quarter- ;4nl in opposition to each other. The neap range is smaller than the mean range for semidiurnal and mixed tides.

Nearshore - In beach terminology, an indefinite zone extending seaward from the shoreline well beyond the breaker zone

Nourishment - Process of replenishing a beach either naturally by longshore transport or artificially by delivery of materials dredged or excavated elsewhere.

Offshore - (1) (Noun) In beach terminology, comparatively flat zone of variable width extending from the breaker zone to the seaward edge of the Continental Shelf. (2) (Adjective) Direction seaward from the shore.

Overtopping - Passing of water over a structure from wave runup or surge action.

Peat - Residual product produced by partial decomposition of organic matter in marshes and bogs.
Peat Pot (vegetation) - Pot formed from compressed peat and filled either with soil or peat moss in which a plant or plants, grown from seed, are transplanted without being removed from the pot.

Perched Beach - Beach or fillet of sand retained above the otherwise normal profile level by a submerged dike or sill.

Permeable - Having openings large enough to permit free passage of appreciable quantities of (1) sand or (2) water.

Pile - Long, heavy section of timber, concrete or metal driven or jetted into the earth or seabed as support or protection.

Pile, Sheet - Pile with a generally slender, flat cross section driven into the ground or seabed and meshed or interlocked with like members to form a diaphragm, wall, or bulkhead.

Piling - Group of piles.

Plug - Core containing both plants and underlying soil, usually cut with a cylindrical coring device and transplanted to a hole cut by the same device.

Polyvinyl Chloride (PVC) - Plastic material (usually black) that forms a resilient coating suitable for protecting metal from corrosion.

Profile, Beach - Intersection of the ground surface with a vertical plane that may extend from the top of the dune line to the seaward limit of sand movement.

PVC - See POLYVINYL CHLORIDE.

Ravelling - Progressive deterioration of a revetment under wave action.

Refraction (of water waves) - (1) Process by which direction of a wave moving in shallow water at an angle to the contours is changed. Part of the wave advancing in shallower water moves more slowly than the part still advancing in deeper water, causing the wave crest to bend toward alignment with the underwater contours. (2) Bending of wave crests by currents.

Revetment - Facing of stone, concrete, etc., built to protect a scarp, embankment, or shore structure against erosion by waves or currents.

Rhizome - Underground stem or root stock. New shoots are usually produced from the tip of the rhizome.

Riprap - Layer, facing, or protective mound of stones randomly placed to prevent erosion, scour, or sloughing of a structure or embankment; also, the stone so used.

Rubble - (1) Loose, angular, waterworn stones along a beach. (2) Rough, irregular fragments of broken rock or concrete.

Runup - The rush of water up a structure or beach on breaking of a wave. Amount of runup is the vertical height above stillwater level that the rush of water reaches.

Sand - Generally, coarse-grained soils having particle diameters between 0.18 and approximately 0.003 inches. Sands are intermediate between SILT and GRAVEL.

Sandbag - Cloth bag filled with sand or grout and used as a module in a shore protection device.

Sand Fillet- Accretion trapped by a groin or other protrusion in the littoral zone.

Scour - Removal of underwater material by waves or currents, especially at the base or toe of a shore structure.

Screw Anchor - Type of metal anchor screwed into the bottom for holding power.

Seawall - Structure separating land and water areas primarily to prevent erosion and other damage by wave action. See also BULKHEAD.

Semidiurnal Tide - Tide with two high and two low waters in a tidal day, each high and each low approximately equal in stage.

Setup, Wind - Vertical rise in the Stillwater level on a body of water caused by piling up of water on the shore due to wind action. Synonymous with wind tide and STORM SURGE. STORM SURGE usually pertains to the ocean and large bodies of water. Wind setup usually pertains to reservoirs and smaller bodies of water.

Shallow Water - Commonly, water of such a depth that surface waves are noticeably affected by bottom topography. It is customary to consider water of depths less than one-twentieth the surface wavelength as shallow water.

Sheet Pile - see PILE, SHEET.

Shoot - Collective term applied to the STEM and leaves, or any growing branch or twig.

Shore - Narrow strip of land in immediate contact with the sea, including the zone between high and low water lines. A shore of unconsolidated material is usually called a beach.

Shoreline - intersection of a specified plane of water with the shore or beach (e.g., the high water shoreline would be the intersection of the plane of mean high water with the shore or beach). Line delineating the shoreline on National Ocean Survey nautical charts and surveys approximates the mean high water line.

Sill - Low offshore barrier structure whose crest is usually submerged, designed to retain sand on its landward side.

Silt - Generally refers to fine-grained soils having particle diameters between 0.003 and 0.00015 inches. Intermediate between CLAY and SAND.

Slope - Degree of inclination to the horizontal. Usually expressed as a ratio, such as 1:25 or 1 on 25, indicating 1-unit vertical rise in 25 units of horizontal distance; or in degrees from horizontal.

Specifications - Detailed description of particulars, such as size of stone , quality of materials, contractor performance, terms, and quality control.
Sprig - Single plant with its roots relatively bare, as pulled apart from a clump and used for transplanting.

Stem - Main axis of a plant, leaf-bearing and flower-bearing, as distinguished from the root-bearing axis.

Stillwater Level - Elevation that the surface of the water would assume if all wave action were absent.

Storm Surge - Rise above normal water level on the open coast due to action of wind on the water surface. Storm surge resulting from a hurricane also includes the rise in level due to atmospheric pressure reduction as well as that due to wind stress. See SETUP, WIND.

Swell - Wind-generated waves traveling out of their generating area. Swell characteristically exhibits a more regular and longer period, and has flatter crests than waves within their fetch.

Tidal Range - Difference in height between consecutive high and low or higher high and lower low) waters. The mean range is the difference in height between mean high water and mean low water. The diurnal range is the difference in height between mean higher high water and mean lower low water. For diurnal tides, the mean and diurnal range are identical. For semidiurnal and mixed tides, the spring range is the difference in height between the high and low waters during the time of spring tides.

Tide - Periodic rising and falling of water resulting from gravitational attraction of the moon, sun and other astronomical bodies acting upon the rotating earth. Although the accompanying horizontal movement of the water resulting from the same cause is also sometimes called tide, it is preferable to designate the latter as tidal current, reserving the name TIDE for vertical movement.

Tide Station - Place at which tide observations are being taken. A primary tide station is a location where continuous observations are taken over a number of years to obtain basic tidal data for the locality. A secondary tide station is operated over a short period of time to obtain data for a specific purpose.

Tie Rod - Steel rod used to tie back the top of a bulkhead or seawall. Also, a U-shaped rod used to tie Sandgrabber blocks together, or a straight rod used to tie Nami Rings together.

Tiller - A plant SHOOT which springs from the root or bottom of the original plant stalk.

Topography - Configuration of a surface, including relief, position of streams, roads, buildings, etc.

Transplant - SHOOT or CULM removed from one location and replanted in another.

Trough of Wave - Lowest part of a waveform between successive crests. Also, that part of a wave below stillwater level.

Updrift - Direction opposite the predominant movement of littoral materials in longshore transport.

Wake (boat) - Waves generated by the motion of a vessel through water.

Wale - Horizontal beam on a bulkhead used to laterally transfer loads against the structure and hold it in a straight alignment.

Waterline - Juncture of land and sea. This line migrates, changing with the tide or other fluctuation in water level. Where waves are present on the beach, this line is also known as the limit of backrush. (Approximately, the intersection of land with Stillwater level.)
Wave - Ridge, deformation, or undulation of the surface of a liquid.

Wave Climate - Normal seasonal wave regimen along a shoreline.

Wave Crest - Highest part of a wave or that part above stillwater level.

Wave Diffraction - See DIFFRACTION.

Wave Direction - Direction from which a wave approaches.

Wave Height - Vertical distance between a crest and the preceding trough.

Wavelength - Horizontal distance between similar points on two successive waves measured perpendicular to the crest.

Wave Period - Time in which a wave crest traverses a distance equal to one wavelength. Time for two successive wave crests to pass a fixed point.

Wave Refraction - See REFRACTION (of water waves).

Wave Steepness - Ratio of wave height to wavelength.

Wave Trough - Lowest part of a wave form between successive crests. Also, that part of a wave below that part of a wave below Stillwater level.

Weep Hole - Hole through a solid revetment, bulkhead, or seawall for relieving pore pressure.

Wind Setup - See SETUP, WIND.

Windward - Direction from which wind is blowing.

Wind Waves - (1) Waves being formed and built up by wind. (2) Loosely, any waves generated by wind.

Wave Direction - Direction from which a wave approaches.

Wave Height - Vertical distance between a crest and the preceding trough.

Wavelenth - Horizontal distance between similar points on two successive waves measured perpendicular to the crest.

Wave Period - Time in which a wave crest traverses a distance equal to one wavelength. Time for two successive wave crests to pass a fixed point.

Wave Refraction - See REFRACTION (of water waves).

Wave Steepness - Ratio of wave height to wavelength.

Wave Trough - Lowest part of a wave form between successive crests. Also, that part of a wave below the Stillwater level.

Weep Hole - Hole through a solid revetment, bulkhead, or seawall for relieving pore pressure.

Wind Setup - See SETUP, WIND.

Windward - Direction from which wind is blowing.

Wind Waves - (1) Waves being formed and built up by wind.   (2) Loosely, any waves generated by wind.

LITERATURE CITED

American Wood Preservers' Association, "Standard C18-77: Standard for Pressure Treated Material in Marine Construction", 1977.

American Wood Preservers Institute, "AWPI Technical Guidelines for Pressure Treated Wood - S2 Bulkheads: Design and Construction -Part I", 1970.

Bertram, G. E., "An Experimental Investigation of Protective Filters", Harvard University Publication 267, January 1940.

Davis, A. P., Jr., "Evaluation of Tying Materials for Floating Tire Breakwaters", Marine Technical Report 54, University of Rhode Island, April 1977.

Giles, M. L. and Eckert, J. W., "Determination of Mooring Load and Transmitted Wave Height for a Floating Tire Breakwater", CETA 79-4, U. S. Army Corps of Engineers, Coastal Engineering Research Center, Ft. Belvoir, Virginia, September 1979.

Hall, J. V., Jr., and Jachowski, R. A., "Concrete Block Revetment Near Benedict, Maryland", MP 1-64, U. S. Army Corps of Engineers,

Coastal Engineering Research Center, Ft. Belvoir, Virginia, January 1964.

Harris, D. L., "Tides and Tidal Datums in the United States", SR 7, U. S. Army Corps of Engineers, Coastal Engineering Research Center, Ft. Belvoir, Virginia, February 1981.

Hobson, R. D., "Review of Design Elements for Beach Fill Evaluation", TP 77-6, U. S. Army Corps of Engineers, Coastal Engineering Research Center, Ft. Belvoir, Virginia, June 1977.

Lambe, T. and Whitman, R. W., *Soil Mechanics,* John Wiley and Sons, Inc., New York, 1969.

Mather, B., "Factors Affecting the Durability of Concrete in Coastal Structures", TM-96, U.S. Army Corps of Engineers, Beach Erosion Board, Washington, D. C., June 1957.

Neill, C. R., "Dynamic Ice Forces on Piers and Piles: An Assessment of Design Guidelines in Light of Recent Research", *Canadian Journal of Civil Engineering,* Vol. 3, 1976, pp. 305-341.

Seelig, W., "Estimation of Wave Transmission Coefficients for Overtopping of Impermeable Breakwaters", CETA 80-7, U. S. Army Corps of Engineers, Coastal Engineering Research Center, Ft. Belvoir, Virginia, December 1980.

Stoa, P. N., "Revised Wave Runup Curves for Smooth Slopes", CETA 78-2, U. S. Army Corps of Engineers, Coastal Engineering Research Center, Ft. Belvoir, Virginia, July 1978.

Stoa, P. N., "Wave Runup on Rough Slopes", CETA 79-1, U. S. Army Corps of Engineers, Coastal Engineering Research Center, Ft. elvoir, Virginia, July 1979.

Thom, H.C.S., "New Distributions of Extreme Winds in the United States", *Journal of the Structural Division,* ASCE, No. ST7, July 1968, pp. 1787-1801.

U.S. Army Corps of Engineers, "Plastic Filter Fabric", civil works Guide Specification CW 02215, Office, Chief of Engineers, Washington, D. C., 1977a.

U.S. Army Corps of Engineers, "Regulatory Program of the Corps of Engineers", *Federal Register,* Vol. 42, No. 138, Washington, D. C., Tuesday, 19 July 1977b.

U. S. Army Corps of Engineers, "Shore Protection Manual", Coastal Engineering Research Center, Ft. Belvoir, Virginia, 1977c.

U.S. Army Corps of Engineers, "Geneva State Park, Ohio, Shore Erosion Control Demonstration Program, Preconstruction Report", Engineer District, Buffalo, February 1978a.

U.S. Army Corps of Engineers, "Pickering Beach, Delaware: Preconstruction Report", Engineer District, Philadelphia, April 1978b.

U.S. Army Corps of Engineers, "Kitts Hummock, Delaware: Preconstruction Report", Engineer District, Philadelphia, April 1978c.

U.S. Army Corps of Engineers, "Help Yourself: A Discussion of Erosion Problems on the Great Lakes and Alternative Methods of Shore Protection", Engineer Division, North Central, September 1978d.

U. S. Army Corps of Engineers, "Bank Erosion Control with Smooth Cordgrass and Saltmeadow Cordgrass on the Atlantic Coast", TN-V-2, Coastal Engineering Research Center, Ft. Belvoir, Virginia, March 1980a.

U.S. Army Corps of Engineers, "Engineering and Design: Ice Engineering", Engineering Circular 1110-2-220, Washington, D. C., October 1980b.

U.S. Army Corps of Engineers, "Monthly Bulletin of Lake Levels for the Great Lakes", Engineer District, Detroit, March 1981a.

U.S. Army Corps of Engineers, "Method of Determining Adjusted Windspeed, U,, for Wave Forecasting", CETN-I-5, Coastal Engineering Research Ceneer, Ft. Belvoir, Virginia, March 1981b.

U.S. Army Corps of Engineers, "Revised Method for Wave Forecasting in Shallow Water", CETN-I-6, Coastal Engineering Research Center, Ft. Belvoir, Virginia, March 1981c.

U.S. Army Corps of Engineers, "Low Cost Shore Protection: Final Report on the Shoreline Erosion Control Demonstration Program," Office, Chief of Engineers,, Washington, D.C., 1981d.

U. S. Department of Commerce, "Tide Tables: High and Low Water Predictions", NOAA, National Ocean Survey, Washington, D. C., 1976.

U S. Navy, Naval Facilities Engineering Command, "Soil Mechanics, Foundations and Earth Structures," NAVFAC DM-7, Washington, D. C., 1971.

United States Steel Corporation, 11 Steel Sheet Piling Design Manual", Pittsburgh, Pennsylvania, 1975.

Watson, L., Machemehl, J. and Barnes, B., "Deterioration of Asbestos Cement Sheet Material in the Marine Environment", *Proceedings of the Coastal Structures 179 Conference,* Vol. I., pp. 230-249, 1979.

Weggel, J. R., "Maximum Breaker Height", *Journal of the Waterways, Harbors and Coastal Engineering Division,* ASCE, Vol. 98, No. WW4, Paper 9384, 1972.

Wiegel, R. L., "Waves, Tides, Currents, and Beaches: Glossary of Terms and List of Standard Symbols", Council on Wave Research, The Engineering Foundation, University of California, 1953.

Winterkorn, H. F., and Fang, H. Y., *Foundation Engineering Hand*book, Van Nostrand Reinhold Company, New York, 1975.

Wortley, C. A., "Ice Engineering Guide for Design and Construction of Small Craft Harbors", Advisory Report No. WIS-SG-78-417, University of Wisconsin, Madison, Wisconsin, 1978.